FORD

AN ERA REMEMBERED

BY
O.J. NORI

FERNE PRESS

Nori, O.J.
Summary: A longtime employee of Ford Motor Company experiences mob influences, works with famous celebrities, and meets Elvis Presley in an autobiographical account of a career spanning some five decades.

Nori, O.J. (1924 –)
Ford: An Era Remembered
ISBN: 978-1-933916-02-6, 1-933916-02-8
1. Ford Motor Company – History. 2 Automobile Industry and Trade – United States. I. Title
Library of Congress Control Number: 2006935279

FERNE PRESS

Ferne Press is an imprint of Nelson Publishing & Marketing
366 Welch Road, Northville, MI 48167
www.nelsonpublishingandmarketing.com
(248) 735-0418

This book is dedicated with love to my family: my wife, Margie; my daughter, Teresa (Punky); her husband, Rick; and our grandchildren: Nicky, Danielle, Alyssa, and Jaymie; all of whom provided that support needed, including the technical advice in this endeavor, to ensure my project was successfully accomplished. My thanks to them and to my parents who guided me from the beginning in steering a steady righteous course toward achieving a realistic objective.

TABLE OF CONTENTS

PREFACE

L
ike many individuals who have at one time or another thought of sitting down and writing a book of their background and experiences, I too have been harboring that thought for some time. I've thought of putting in writing the many and varied experiences I personally have witnessed and experienced, and more than once, asked myself the question and wondered whether it would be best told in book form, and whether there are those who would possibly enjoy the reading, understand the innermost meanings, and accept a share of the knowledge. While repeatedly setting aside the recall and writing effort, procrastinating as time went on, and occupied by other unrelated and mundane priorities of daily living, there was always the thought that there nonetheless was a story to be told. I was finally prompted to get down to the initial writing while in the hospital, and the recall and writing assisted in passing countless hours, and for all purposes assisted in getting me back to good health.

For those of you beginning to read this book and trying to understand where it would lead, let me set the scenario straight. What we have in this book is a true and factual portrayal from personal memory, spanning a period of greater than five decades. This is what and how it happened. Hopefully, this factual portrayal of one's major slice of life may shed light on its realities and guide others in gaining a better understanding of the actualities of life, gaining thereby a more comprehensive knowledge in the development and pursuit of their own individual lives, ambitions, and careers.

Unlike a personalized autobiographical accounting of life, that which follows is the actual and factual experience of a proud young man — an individual who, in fact, dedicated himself to the task of preparing and hanging on to a lone objective and hanging on until that challenging objective was accomplished. This determined tenaciousness spanned a prolonged time period and simultaneously provided an insight of the times to the many related happenings. I was greatly privileged to be there, to participate in those many happenings, and to actually participate in retrospect in what today is considered "the making of history."

CHAPTER 1
BROTHER, CAN YOU SPARE A DIME?

It all began in the years of the Great Depression. Life was peaceful and tranquil for a youngster who had all he knew of life: his parents, family, and grandparents. There was also the vegetable garden I was every so often responsible for, the rabbits I had to make sure were fed, and the lawn requirements when my dad instructed me on what to do. As youngsters within our family circle, all of our chores were well defined and understood. While most of the time was spent in family-oriented requirements, there were many opportunities to spend enjoying and growing up in our family circle and in the company of my grandfather as well. He enjoyed our togetherness as much as we enjoyed being with him and doing the many kid things he knew we liked.

Like most men of the time, my grandfather didn't have work and had to busy himself doing many odd jobs in the neighborhood for small pay. I tried to help in the small paint jobs and fence repairs, as well as cleaning out the pigeon coops when asked to assist. Interesting is the fact that I learned how to handle the tools and find myself using that knowledge today. I knew that once the little chores were done, the rest of the time would be spent in our personal explorations and travels. Between our work activities we stopped many times at some small shops and the like, seeking possible day work. It is difficult to relay how many different places we visited asking if there was work or the possibility of work then or in the near future. Because of the times, it seemed that no matter how hard we tried there was no work to be had. More often than not we would come across others looking for some sort of work as well. It was not uncommon for me to be asked by a passing stranger if I had a nickel or something to eat. It's hard to imagine by today's way of life, but for those who may yet recall, that's how desperate and trying it was for many. People were hungry.

I vividly recall the many trips my grandfather and I made to the Ford Motor Company on Miller Road in the Dearborn, Michigan area. We'd walk from home to Gate 1 on Fort Street, and on to Gate 4 where the Battle of the Overpass was eventually fought, which, in fact, was the prelude to the continuing battle between the Ford Motor Company and the UAW-CIO, eventually ending in a contract between the parties. There were hundreds of men just milling around and waiting for some signs of being signaled toward the entry gate for an employment opportunity. We'd more often than not end up at Gate 2 where the main center of activity existed. Our travels to the Gate 2 area would take us across many fields, around what were then large brickyards, deep ravines, and the quicksand areas, all of which were in the southern Dearborn area. Once we got past the

The eight famous Ford smokestacks.

cemeteries and the little shops along our way, the eight famous Ford smokestacks were in sight. At that point, no employment possibilities existed between home and the Ford Motor Company. There was always the hope something would develop, perhaps at Ford. We had already checked the rail sidings, coming and going to the little shops, on our way to Ford, and if the rails were rusted it was obvious there was no activity going on at the facility. There was no point in asking about, waiting, or seeking employment at such facilities. We covered miles of shoe leather checking out any possibility and frequently repeating the travel path more often than I can recall.

Once we arrived at the Ford Motor Company, hundreds of men seemed to be walking around aimlessly, all hoping a Ford service man (a plant guard in today's terms) would come to the gate and allow a few people in. When this happened there was a mad rush to get to the gate where it appeared some activity was taking place. The police and the Ford service people just pushed people, some falling and obviously hurt, others pushed by the horses the Dearborn police rode on. It was complete bedlam, and this was repeated over and over until there was no daylight left. It's difficult to put into writing the desperation and unbelievable anxiety of so many just to get an honest job, to earn some money regardless of how little, just to feed their family.

I watched all this from the curbside seat my grandfather had assigned me to, and it was scary to watch. There never was the concern as to where I would go should my granddad be fortunate enough to be selected to go into the employment office. The attitude that seemed to prevail was that nothing would come of this exercise, and we would be on our way home in a little while. If the possibility ever came to pass that a job was being made available, there was always a friend or neighbor who would gladly assist in seeing to it that I got back safely. It was common for so many friends and neighbors to be seeking an opportunity for a job.

I've mentioned the police with their horses trying to control the masses, pushing and shoving the men back away from the entrance areas and often knocking them down into the muddy side areas for what appeared to be no reason whatever. On one of these occasions, my

The Gate 2 area.

granddad came back to where I was sitting. He was pretty much muddied up and embarrassed of his condition. Again my thoughts centered on "why." Why were they causing this to happen? He was an honest man, as were the others, and all they wanted was an opportunity to work, to buy food for their families. If I could ever get beyond the guards and into the offices, I recall thinking many times, I would most certainly do things differently, thinking one day somehow I would. This is where it all began. This was not, as I remember, some young kid dreaming or wishing it could happen, nor was it merely a passing thought, but rather a promise I was making to myself that something should and would be done. I would not let these people and police do what they were doing but rather give these people seeking employment an opportunity to talk to someone and give them hope that perhaps they may have an opportunity at some later time. Once returning home, we busied ourselves with the chores left undone and thereafter joined my uncles and their friends sitting on the front porch listening to the ballgame.

Baseball was a big thing at the time and because not many could afford a radio, my grandfather's radio was turned up loud so that all could hear, including those passing by. It was something to behold listening to Ty Tyson calling the balls and strikes and the repeated reference to Mobil Gas and the Flying Red Horse. If it wasn't the ballgame they listened to, the group was out on the sandlots playing the game. My uncle Ed, a good softball pitcher, led the league in strikeout pitching.

The team, as I recall, was sponsored by a local business enterprise whose name was Tager Machine Motor Parts. My dad, grandfather, and as many as could fit into a Graham-Paige car that belonged to the family, all went to the weekly games. All others walked approximately two miles and back. These were the good times for a youngster, and learning as life went on.

Kelsey Hayes, a local wheel and drum manufacturing facility that, like so many other firms, was dependent on the automobile industry, had laid off their complement of employees. My grandfather was one of the many who had lost his source of income as a result. He waited anxiously for a postal card or word from Kelsey's that he would be returned to work. He eventually got a call to return and even though the opportunity was for a day or two a week, he was very happy to gain at least some income. I watched and waited for him on the days he worked, when he would return tired and dirty. He never complained of the dirt, dust, and sweat of the job and seemed to be pleased to see me on the corner, as I was to see him.

Bright and early in the morning on those days he wasn't required to report for work, I could hear his whistle from across the street from our home, my signal to meet him. Unbeknown to me, the arrangement had already been made with my parents, and they were well aware of what was to take place. My customary lunch for two was wrapped in newspaper and on the front porch. My exiting was out the bedroom window, down the front steps, and on my way, as my mother or dad called to be careful and pick up my lunch as I left. I knew we would have a good time but wasn't sure the direction we'd take. When we waited at the streetcar stop for the six-cent streetcar to come, I already knew we would be heading for the downtown area and the small theaters, most of which were showing cowboy movies. These were our favorites. We had the selection of Tom Mix, Ken Maynard, and many other western movies, all of which cost a dime and children half price. We usually went to more than one, stopping only to eat a part of our lunch on the way. My granddad couldn't hear or understand what was going on very well, and it was my job to interpret what was being said, talking loud enough for him to understand. Much of our communication was at the expense of some of the other persons watching the movie, and they would frequently let us know we were bothering them.

CHAPTER 2
GATE 2: THE EMPLOYMENT OFFICE

It wasn't too many months later that my family decided to move from the old neighborhood to Dearborn. There were several reasons for the move, one being the bank suddenly making a demand for greater monthly payment for the house we had lived in for years, located very near my grandparents' home. The banking laws were quite loose and it was not uncommon for a homeowner to get a demand for a change in their account, bordering on an eviction. With only four thousand dollars left to pay on the principal, which was a considerable amount of money at the time, my father decided not to bend to the wishes of the bank, even though, after the fact, they made repeated requests to withdraw their former demand and return to the prior payment arrangement. So we moved out. The balance the bank sought at an increased interest rate was not compatible with what one could purchase a new home for. This was cause enough for the bank officials to realize their actions were not financially prudent, nor could they convince my mother or dad to remain. After we moved out, I recall the property was left vacant, which was not an uncommon sight in many of the neighborhoods. In effect, the greediness of the bank officials caused them to have a piece of property vacant and no return, while we were fortunate enough to move to a much newer home in an upscale neighborhood with greater potential for the future. I recently had occasion to drive back through the old neighborhood and saw that the house we had grown up in had burned down to the ground. This didn't surprise me as the property had been in complete disarray and in need of what appeared to be major repair. While there were still other good reasons to make the move, the other significant reason was job security while living in the Dearborn area. My previous monthly trips to the bank, with the monthly mortgage envelope money pinned inside my undershirt, would no longer be required.

Even though we moved to the Dearborn area, my dad was working only intermittently at Ford. The likelihood of recall to his Ford job was much greater as a resident of the city. His work retention opportunity was better than most, as he was a big, strong, hard-working man. His beginnings and tough learnings were traced to the Pennsylvania coal mines. He endowed himself with a good work reputation, and, if not called back to his normal job, the plant guards making the employment selection would pick him because of his size. Fortunately, like the sign of the times and like many others, he never paid for a job as did many others at the time, nor did he have to wine and dine the scum that flaunted their acquaintance or association with those at the Ford hiring desk as a means of getting a job. Here again was the situation where graft and payoffs ran rampant. A card with the name of one of the insiders at the Ford hiring desk was an automatic opportunity at the hiring gates for employment. It was known by many that an ordinary production job would cost an applicant about fifty dollars, a non-production job much more, and a maintenance assignment, practically without skill, a small fortune. The main payoff location that almost guaranteed a job and hiring almost by day's end was a small neighborhood grocery store in the shadows of the Rouge plant. While there were many others involved in the "pay for a job" ruse, the main circle was within the Dearborn south end. A quick example without going into detail was the cons being worked on the inside of the office, i.e., you sign up for a new car and I'll get you a job. Another was the slippery insurance salesman: buy from me instead of a company insurance policy, and you get a job. The tie-in was, once you accepted the offer, the selling person had your name, address, and names of your family members, giving him carte blanche entry into your personal life for additional insurance sales—you or they got the insurance coverage, he got the commissions, and the company got cleverly bypassed. These were two of the many scams that were taking place all with a dollar payoff in one fashion or another by those within the office or with direct ties to the individuals within the Gate 2 employment office. Small fortunes were being made and those involved were very protective of their scam and of their territory. The *sotto manne*, or underhanded activity, was obvious to many, but because of overlapping involvement, management was neither doing nor saying anything to stop the brazen activity.

My grandfather would come visiting our Dearborn residence often, now that we had moved a distance away. I'd go out to meet him at the streetcar stop and we'd talk all the way back home, retelling our stories since our last meeting. He always had a small parcel for our family — the girls would get candy or chocolate and for me it was either a large Hershey bar or a fifty-cent piece. We all knew what he would be doing and appreciated it very much. I've since learned from Margie, my wife, that she too recalls him visiting with her family every now and then and each time he did, he always had as a trademark a large bar of Hershey chocolate. At our home, we made a game of keeping what we got a secret. We were a small family in comparison to most during the Depression and we watched out for one another. Sharing was the word and no *scustomati*, which in Italian we understood to mean not taking more than your share; more than your share would not be tolerated. This has been passed down even today where the grandkids refer to one taking more than his or her own share as "scush," and that reference is well understood by all.

Irene was the oldest and she quite capably guided our activities, then me, Marian, and Dina. Bernice, the youngest, was born in our Detroit house just before we moved to Dearborn. Johnny was a late arrival and a good one in the family, born after I had left for the service. My visits back to the old neighborhood became less frequent because my responsibilities within the family became greater. Nonetheless, my grandfather kept up with his visits and made it a point to sit with my dad over a glass of wine and a game of Briscola, a variation of the American card game gin. His visits provided the opportunity to meet him at the streetcar stop when arriving as well as walking him back, talking about our past happenings, and setting our plans for the future. My thoughts almost always centered on how much happier he would be if he had the opportunity to gain employment at Ford, or steady employment anywhere.

CHAPTER 3
TIME FOR A CHANGE

The early beginnings in our new home in Dearborn were a difficult transition for the whole family. Employment for my dad was unsteady, no telephone—because of the added expense—made transportation arrangements hard to come by, and this was the period we lost Dina, the second youngest member of our family, due to illness. We moved several times after her passing, for it was difficult for both my parents to be living in the house where the funeral had been held. Funerals were, by custom and experience of the times, held at the home.

To ensure the house payments were met, the food was adequate, and clothing was there for all of us, my mother, over the strong objections of my dad, took a small job at a local restaurant to supplement the family income. The times were difficult, but as youngsters, we were not caused to suffer. In addition to the income from her small job at the restaurant, my mother also was expert in knitting and sewing and again supplemented the family fund by taking orders and filling them on quick demand. The youngest member, Johnny, wasn't yet born, and to this day I wonder whether he would have benefited by our experiences during those few years, or if he was better off just falling into the good times. I'm glad he did miss the period, and there's proof of his well-being, as he became a successful doctor, and had a lovely wife and three children, two of whom also became doctors.

My next ten years or so were spent in school, preparing for whatever was to come. I learned early that backgrounds in business and commercial subjects were essential if one sought assignment at Ford. I drifted in that direction for an education. No one in our family was of a college background, nor were there funds to promote such thinking. We all knew that and regardless of our personal desires we never questioned the situation. My grandfather passed away during this period and I became very ill as a result of his death and couldn't even attend the funeral.

I was fortunate in my adolescent years for possessing a strong understanding of some of life's pitfalls and the direction necessary to avoid the traps while striving for personal understanding and improvement. As a result of my achievement in the commercial field while attending my freshman year at high school, I, along with about five others in a class of approximately three hundred, was given the opportunity to qualify for a sponsored cooperative program. The co-op was under the direction of a large utility within the community and the board of education. At fourteen, I was on the payroll at a weekly income of fifteen dollars a week, and on a semi-monthly schedule—two weeks of work and two weeks of school. The pay was great for a youngster and the work was even better. I was assigned to a message center unit, given a fresh white shirt every day, and made aware that my retention was based solely on my ability to maintain a high scholastic average and by abiding by the requirements of my employment. The various managers in the areas I was assigned to had also the responsibility to assure that I and other co-op student-employees would open our school books when the work in the office slowed down.

Fifteen dollars twice monthly, or fifteen dollars per week, was a very good income for a youngster. To give you some idea of how much this really was, my dad and I would travel to the east-side market some fifteen miles from home, by public transportation, shopping for groceries for the family for a week. The usual dollar amount for the groceries, which included two large shopping bags full, and frequently one or more live chickens, believe this or not, was just five dollars for the entire family, versus the fifteen dollars I was being paid for a week.

My employment offered me the job of jobs: clean atmosphere, good pay, and the opportunity to be in the company of some of the major executives of the community and industry. This was all pre-war and the learning experience couldn't have been better. Our work activity, as I said before, was programmed on a cooperative basis between school and work. It was co-op in the sense that we went to school two weeks and swung over to work the other two weeks. Our retention was being watched by both the school administrators as well as the Edison utility management, which was responsible for the program. Failing at either end was automatic program removal. Fortunately, I and the several others initiated into the program all survived. I was appreciative of the opportunity, as was my dad, who was proud to see me making my way in life, as was my whole family. I wasn't about to jeopardize what I had, nor was I about to bring shame to myself and family by failing at either school or work. The rapid maturing became obvious. As a consequence, a normal three-year high school attendance requirement was achieved, as a part-time attendee, in one and one-half years.

Mr. Alex Dow was the president of Detroit Edison at the time and appeared to me to be a fine elderly gentleman. People seemed to shy away as he came down the corridors. I saw him rather lonely in this maze of humanity, with a high-stepping cadre close behind, all of whom were positioning to get in an alignment of favored recognition. Mr. Dow's exodus from the building at quitting time was like clockwork. He would be accompanied by his chauffeur who assisted him. They'd come down the freight elevator, and as he passed my area I always received a friendly nod, which I would accordingly acknowledge and return without uttering a word as he was assisted to his waiting car.

I had the feeling Mr. Dow knew what we were doing behind the scenes in our little coffee arrangement, behind the backdrops of our mailing activities. We guessed he could smell the fresh coffee we were brewing as he hobbled by with his cane to his car. He never said a thing nor did we hear any negatives from our superiors on our little secret coffee and pie arrangement. We didn't have a cafeteria for a morning or afternoon break time, in fact there were no breaks considered at the time. Most of the young people frequented a little grocery store next to our building with a little counter for coffee and grabbed their coffee and donuts on the run. The older clientele would either brown-bag their coffee in a thermos for an occasional sip or go without.

Mr. Dow liked his coffee as well, as we later found out through our talks with his chauffeur. Understanding it would be quite improper, if not an intrusion, to come right out and ask if he would like a cup of our daily fresh-brewed coffee and a slice of fresh pie from our totally inconspicuous coffee setting, I felt no harm would come if I'd ask his chauffeur to intervene. We had a chair and small table behind the pigeonhole mail files and while one could see out, you couldn't see in. The area accommodated but one person, the coffee pot, and several varieties of pie. We obtained the pies fresh daily from Mrs. Wagner's pie company which was approximately a block's distance away. The delivery drivers from Mrs. Wagner's were very cooperative with us, as they set aside each pie that had its wrapping slightly torn as a consequence of loading on to their trucks early each morning. Sometimes I think they caused a tear in the wrappings intentionally, understanding who we were and what we were doing. The responsibility of keeping our area very clean as well as changing the coffee grounds and assuring no mess was created was shared between my friend Leo Bemben and myself. There was no collecting of money, but rather a small cash box for donations as the users left. Leo lives in northern Michigan now with his family. I know he'll remember, as I do, the beautiful relationship and experience with Mr. Dow, the president of the company.

It got to a point that our hand and arm signals were thoroughly understood between ourselves and Mr. Dow's chauffeur, when the area was not in use and it was okay for him to bring in Mr. Dow for his morning coffee. Eventually it became known by all that a certain time was reserved for Mr. Dow, and no others should come in. His chauffeur at our entryway was sufficient signal for others to hold off. As indicated, we kept the area clean, there was no nonsense in the area, and no interruptions to the required daily work schedules. We felt Mr. Dow knew this and of our enterprising approach to something less than a totally acceptable practice. We got to a point that we could anticipate his arrival. Once the freight elevator doors swung open and his chauffeur assisted him to our area, he quietly had his coffee, watched what was going on, and left. We didn't say anything nor did he. The business arrangement we had set up as becoming very profitable. Our expenses included the purchase of the coffee and napkins, and the pies were free. We frequently split up the proceeds at about two to three dollars a week. This was a substantial amount of extra money at the time, when you we were making fifteen dollars a week, and this supplement went a long way. We were growing up fast and conducted ourselves in a business-like and respect-able fashion.

The policy of the company at the time was that anyone electing to leave their employment would not be rehired. In other words, once processed for hire, you could retain your work status for as long as you wished. Termination was related solely to voluntary termination on one's part, release because of misconduct, violating your employment agreement, or outright discharge for theft and insubordination. Those employed had the benefit of working in an excellent environment, paid vacations, and insurance benefits. For the most part, the wages to the employees were frozen. Related working conditions and benefits were considered adequate to maintain a strong complement of employees. However, it wasn't long before the employment picture on the outside afforded greater opportunity, both for income as well as advancement. Within a year, the corporate employment policy for Edison was less than alluring and the company was, because of the outside competi-tion, forced to change its employment policy. The com-petition, because of World War II, was everywhere. I thought of my situation for months on end. I knew I had a good job, and everything about the company was right with me. However, I had to weigh two things, one of which was the promise I had made to try somehow to get into the Ford Motor Company, and secondly to do this before Uncle Sam got any closer to calling me to service. The time for a transition for better wages and job opportunity was apparent and I had to make the move. It was either then or never. I chose to approach Mr. Kerr, my supervisor, and inform him of my thinking and plans before entering the service. He accepted the rationale and wished me well.

The two gentlemen that I was fortunate to have had an association with were Mr. Alex Dow, on the left, President of the Detroit Edison Company; the man who accepted my invitation for coffee in our little secret hideaway in the corner of the office and out of sight of the passersby. The other, Mr. Henry Ford himself who, in my opinion, was a gentleman with the welfare of his employees uppermost in his way of life. My association as an employee of his company for forty-two years was and is my testimonial to this great man.

CHAPTER 4
THE EARLY BEGINNINGS

I was confident of my abilities, and people-wise, my commercial background served me well during this and subsequent periods. To put my abilities up front in my search for greater opportunities, I registered with the Michigan Employment Placement Offices. This was the avenue best traveled at the time for placement. This approach worked very well for me. In short order I was called for a scheduled administrative test, which included typing speed and accuracy. Remember, jobs at this time were plentiful and available, however, a prerequisite was a passing score on the test. The other job entry approach was via a friend or a strong acquaintance who had the ability to recommend you for an open position. I had no one in this category. My best bet was to qualify under the direction of the State Agency, and then present my credentials attesting to the level of my capability. Absent such endorsement via the State, my opportunity was zero to none for suitable job placement. These were the times and actually how things were. I submitted my request for testing.

The testing was conducted in what I recall was a fishbowl-like area, with a platform at a higher level circling those being tested. There were no electric typewriters, let alone computers as we have today. The Underwoods, Remingtons, and Royals were the machines of the time. There may have been other units, but these were the ones I knew of. While I was familiar with the characteristics of each, my preference was the Underwood. This machine was my favorite in that we were fortunate to own one in our household, using it for letter writing for my parents, and particularly for our school assignments. Uncle Ed, the baseball pitcher whom I mentioned earlier, was the main catalyst for our Underwood typewriter purchase, as he graduated from Cass Tech valedictorian of his graduating class, and excelled in commerce. We sought his recommendations in such areas.

We had the opportunity to select the typewriter of our choice before starting with the testing. My thinking was not only to select an Underwood, but beyond that as I recall, to position myself adjacent to or behind a proficient speed typist, and in that way I could better pace and surpass the speed, without giving thought to possible errors. As it turned out, it was going to be one of two persons I had set my sights on to race with. I sensed it would be a young lady as I observed her typing from the corner of my eye. She, too, was working with an Underwood and that's all I needed. She shot out of the blocks like a real speedster. If I concentrated on the movement and return of her typing carriage, passing her speed as we moved along, I felt confident I could beat her and in that way accomplish my goal.

Fortunately I succeeded in this little game, unbeknown to my competitor, and I passed the testing with flying colors, as she had as well. I often think of this lovely lady who helped my put my best foot forward, for the best speed typing test score recorded for the Michigan Placement testing facility. We both scored in the high sixties for a fifteen-minute test with one or two errors. The State records can and will attest to that.

As a consequence of the test results, I was afforded the opportunity for job interviews at several of the interviewing stations set up during a subsequent recruiting fair. I was still seventeen and recently graduated from high school. I selected several openings that I thought would be interesting, including one with the Packard Motor Car Company. As I had expected, all was well with the potential employers until it came to the question of my age, thereby nullifying any possibility of hire. There was, however, one who examined my credentials and asked if I'd be interested in part-time employment working with their company. The movie production studio was, as I recall it, MGM, Metro-Goldwyn-Mayer, that was making the offer. It could have been even Warner Brothers, but at this time, I'm not sure which one it was. Anyway, the offer was right, including cab fare to and from designated theaters, one meal, and a flat wage. No mention was made of age nor did I volunteer the information. I was assigned the motion picture *The Pride of the Yankees*, where it would be playing, date and time. Gary Cooper was the lead, portraying Lou Gehrig.

My job was to record the attendance, young and old, male and female, listen for comments regarding likes or dislikes, and in the main critique and record the attendees' reactions to the movie: the cast and any factors deemed worthy of appraising the parent company of, i.e., dish night, local competition, etc. The on-site work was interesting but negligible. That which took considerable time was the completion of the packet of forms, required to be completed and submitted directly to Hollywood, on a timely basis. As I think back, I covered the movie at most Detroit and metropolitan locations to the point of sheer monotony with almost knowing the lines of each actor, the good features and the bad. My reports were considered highly acceptable by the Hollywood people, and my checks were coming in regularly.

It wasn't long thereafter that I received a call asking if I would consider full-time employment coupled with travel through several states. A car was necessary, and they would pay for the related expenses, as well as a substantial pay increase. I thought of the offer for some time before giving them my answer. I informed them a series of conflicts stood in my way for an affirmative answer. For one thing there was no certainty of job duration, no insurance and related benefits, and above all was the desire on my part for career employment before entering the service. Because of the war there was still ample opportunity to search out stable and better paying employment.

I had learned that if one qualified, seventeen was an acceptable age for administrative work at Ford. As such, I headed for the Ford Motor Company general offices, where I again was tested and, having passed the tests, was referred to several locations for placement. Luck was again on my side, as I was acceptable for placement at the Gate 2 employment, exactly the location I desired from the beginning. Remember this was the area which in my mind was so controversial to me. This was the area where hungry men were being pushed around a few short years before, and those with authority cared less of their honest desires for work. I was certain that if faith stayed with me, eventually I might fulfill my promise to change the way people looking for employment at Ford were being treated. The story doesn't end with this commitment for employment—there was still the processing to be completed, along with the physical examination, and other employment-related forms to be processed.

I was stopped cold in my tracks at one of the final processing stages. Mr. Jim Kenny was his name. He examined all my credentials, as he peered down his nose through a pair of Benjamin Franklin glasses. He shook his little bald head, and said he was not authorized to accept my job bid, because of my birth certificate. I explained that the certificate served me well in all instances, and no one had ever questioned its validity. His comment was that while the document looked proper it lacked the state of Pennsylvania's embossed seal. The seal was imprinted but not embossed. Obviously I was put out, based on what appeared to be fly-specking on his part, and requested his recommendation. He wanted an embossed seal and that seemed to be the long and short of it. In short order I collected my thinking, asking if he could withhold his conclusions until I had the opportunity to adjust the situation. Can you imagine what I was going through? Here after all these years of hoping upon hope, I finally succeeded in getting to the stepping stone of where I wanted to be, and here because of what I thought to be a technicality was this little man calling the shots against my life's ambitions. I was beside myself but again refrained from losing my composure and sought a solution.

I asked Mr. Kenny if he would consider a week's delay before rejecting my employment forms. Obviously this type of questioning had never occurred to him before. I told him if I wasn't back in the time limit allowed, he could do what he had to do. My plan was to some way, somehow get the required seal via the Pennsylvania state capital and bring him the certificate he sought. His reaction seemed to be one of being caught off guard and, sensing the need for compassion, he reluctantly agreed to my plan.

CHAPTER 5
A PERIOD OF TRANSITION

I had fourteen dollars in my wallet, more than enough to get me to Pennsylvania by rail. I called home, told my parents what had taken place, and that I planned to go directly to the state capital in Harrisburg and get the needed credentials. I was aware this would not be an easy task, and to try obtaining the certificate via the mails was hopeless. This I knew for a fact as I had an aunt slightly older than myself who had already waited more than six months for an adjusted confirmation from the state. I asked my parents to forward some clothing, as well as extra money should I run into difficulty, directing them to mail it to Pittsburgh general delivery. I was determined to follow through with my plan and my dad acknowledged the urgency without hesitating. Much to my surprise, he instructed me to seek out an old acquaintance in the Pittsburgh area who would assist. The man's name was Sam Cammarata, and he owned a restaurant and bar on Peppermint Drive. All I recall was that our family had helped him out at a very crucial time in his life, and he would willingly assist in any way possible. I was in Pennsylvania in short order, located the address given to me on Peppermint Drive, and found Mr. Cammarata. My plans were proceeding as I had hoped. To my surprise, after relating the whole story of my assorted events, I was told not to worry and he, Mr. Cammarata, would handle the situation. His two sons had checked me out of my hotel, the situation was taken completely out of my hands, and I was told to be patient, as things from their end would be taken care of. I had my breakfast, lunch, and dinner at their restaurant for the next several days, always showing my anxiety for a quick resolution to my predicament.

Never having met Mr. Cammarata before, I got the immediate impression he was a patient and decent person. Frequented by many city officials, police, and the press, he had the restaurant and bar in a good location. He had the reputation of helping wherever he could. He was not looking for favors from anyone but seemed to be handling his affairs openly and honestly. I was pleased that my dad had helped this man many years before, the circumstances of which I was not acquainted with nor did I ask. In any event his quick response, after I related my plight, indicated he well recalled the obligation, and would help. This was a very long waiting period for me. That evening at dinner, Mr. Cammarata assured me he had forwarded my certificate to the proper authorities who were in routine contact with those responsible, and I would have the embossed seal soon. His promise was good, and in three days he handed me the certificate with the required seal. After many thanks, I was on my way to the train station and on my way back to Ford. The main leg of my journey, thanks to the Cammarata family, was accomplished.

It wasn't until sometime later that I was able to piece together what and how this was done. I found out that my records were given to the police agency having to do with arrested convicts and the like and they had direct and immediate requiring response from the corresponding agency at the state capital. They would authenticate records of the named individuals and return the forms properly embossed, notarized, and returned to the requesting agency. This was a high-priority processing requirement. In effect, if I had gone the route of delayed handling, as Aunt Flora was experiencing, I most assuredly would have waited a considerable time longer and missed what I knew to be my golden opportunity. By being processed as a felon, incarcerated with other prisoners whose records required state review and authentication, the response time was quick and complete. Obviously, I was put in this group, processed, and thankful the system had such an arrangement. By the way, Aunt Flora received confirmation shortly thereafter. A letter accompanying her embossed certificate indicated there had been a fire during the year of concern and many of the records were destroyed. This didn't answer my concern relative to a lacking embossed seal but why care once the situation was corrected?

I had been initially issued a paper badge for my return entry by Mr. Kenny and, as a consequence, had no problem with re-entry once arriving at Gate 2. The guard acknowledged the badge and waived me past the waiting lineup. I went right to the area and desk where my papers were, uncertain that they were still available. To my surprise, my presence didn't spark the recall from Mr. Kenny that I had expected, but I quickly dismissed the apparent memory loss, knowing I was operating at top speed mentally, and most certainly he wasn't tracking with me. His desk area was covered with people's processing forms, and he seemed to be operating at a much slower pace than I was. I dismissed the thought, concluding it must have been age and debility on his part and I wanted only to get down to the question: what had he done with my papers. I reintroduced myself to Mr. Kenny and got in return what appeared to be a courteous acknowledgement. He didn't know who I was, and I was dying on the vine. I reminded him of our understanding and pointed to the bottom drawer where I saw he had put my papers. He appeared, as he bent down, to seriously search for my papers, but I knew in my mind that he was just going through an exercise. I spotted my papers in the bottom of his drawer and pointed this out to him, practically directing his hand where it was to go. Finally we got there, he pulled out the mess of papers, reread the forms, and apparently recall crept in. He signed my papers, stamped them okay, and directed me to the photographic department for my record picture. This was the end of Mr. Kenny for me, and the end of a very bad initial dream, which ultimately was rectified and made to be a blessing.

After photographic, I wasn't certain where to go. There really wasn't an established routing nor exact directions. I was savvy enough to keep my mouth shut and await direction—someone was sure to tell what was next. As I finalized the processing prerequisites, I had a job—doing what or where I wasn't certain. What was obvious was the employment office appeared to be in completely disorganized array, with many bodies coming and going and still others just standing around taking in all of the commotion. There seemed, on the other hand, to be many odd and unsavory characters in the midst of all the confusion, just standing and observing as well. I wasn't about to call attention to my curiosity by raising question as to their duties or responsibilities. I had a job, right in the middle of the arena that I wanted to become a part of, and interestingly enough, amongst those I had heard of, for the better part of life, as "the makers of kings."

If I recall the time period, I applied for work sometime in July 1942, shortly after leaving school. I was still seventeen. Money was not the object. I knew I'd get a proper starting wage and given the opportunity I would progress. I was assigned as an employment representative. Salary was at seventy-five cents per hour, eight hours per day and five days a week. Insurance, vacation, and the like were all included. My take-home pay would be around one hundred dollars per month after deductions. That was big money for the times and for me. I realized that whether I failed because of circumstances beyond my control or succeeded from the stepping stone provided, I had accomplished what I had promised to myself, and wasn't about to screw up.

My father and I compared notes, and while he was working at a semi-skilled job, our income wasn't that much different. My friends either didn't have employment or they had menial gas station work, or were employed as bus boys and the like. There wasn't anything wrong with such assignments—in this very confused time period, they were fortunate to have the income. My whole family was proud of the happenings and emphasized the Italian proverb, "*Fa bene e scordade, fa male e pendice.*" Translated, "Do good and forget about it, do bad and think about it." This is the doctrine we lived by and even to this time it still exists with us.

It's very difficult to put into proper perspective the attitudes that prevailed then versus now. Those within the office selfishly guarded their little domain very tight-lipped and unwilling to communicate. Their guarded attitudes appeared to be a protective veil for their personal job security. The only response was to their supervisor when asked, flaunting their supposed in-depth knowledge in the area of question. The personnel that had assignments were very dedicated to their responsibilities, while on the other hand, I couldn't help but wonder, who were all the others, looking like undercover persons merely hanging around and doing nothing. Their presence seemed to be tolerated by the supervisors, so who was I to question their presence?

In all the confusion that existed, I still didn't know what I was to do, and so I awaited direction and instruction. I was eventually directed to the office of a middle-aged man, very neatly attired, and he in turn escorted me to the office of his superior. This was Mr. A.J. Miller, the manager of the Ford personnel department. I knew who he was, as his name had been bandied around amongst our friends and acquaintances as a most important Ford executive. The purpose of my being directed to Mr. Miller by Mr. Tom Silvester was to serve as an interview and orientation of what I would do. It wasn't much of a meeting as I recall. He was, however, very much a gentleman and welcomed my presence in the employment office. Again I was passed along to Mr. Silvester, who played a very key role in the employment office. I later learned he was the sole individual responsible for my being hired and it was through his recommendations that I was accepted for hire. From that time on, he guided my every move within the office, tolerated me, and through it all, he was my benefactor from a distance, and whose past friendship I'll cherish always. Initially my assignments were made on an as-needed basis. While to many this would have been an undesirable situation, I benefited greatly by getting a full understanding of the many entwined tasks, participating in the decision-making, and from time to time being asked for my opinion or actually participating in the concluding determination. This is something for the younger generation to understand — you can't become a king of the hill without fully understanding what the basics consists of and how to act or react properly when the occasion arises. As time went by I found that supervision would come directly to me for answers. If they were not acquainted with the process, whether before or after, and needed a quick determination, they sought me out for the answer. I must have earned a good reputation for quick and understandable answers. I was enjoying the position I was being put into and looked forward to what the next day's activity would bring. To a great extent there was no point in attempting to gain the knowledge and experience by asking those within. Unfortunately, those within, supervisors or managers, didn't have or know the answers. Intentionally or otherwise, I found times where I was being misdirected. I had to learn this, and at times found myself being improperly advised and learned to avoid those participating in such tactics. To participate in real situations, such as interpreting record data, providing status on insurance files, compensation claims, and above all one's job and seniority status, and the like, I studied the situation thoroughly, spoke to those I learned to have confidence in, got to understand the issue or problem area, and could quite readily provide the right answers when asked.

These were the war years, the waiting area and the people lineup were everywhere within the office, as well as the lineups outdoors all waiting or hoping to enter the building. Everyone within seemed to be heading in different directions to get done whatever they came into the office for. People were being hired, others transferring between one of the many plant buildings and or jobs, and others being terminated. The con men were working their games in the office, and the plant guards at the entrance gate had their little thing going in the form of directing young ladies who were driving up to the gate for employment to remote places in the adjacent huge parking lots for personal sexual favors, before referring them in for an employment interview. As a matter of fact, I recall recognizing a certain lady from the metropolitan area who would make her frequent visits to the office always with a male companion in hand. The obvious conclusion was that she had what appeared to be automatic entry into the office, unlike most, and accomplished her mission of referring her companions to the right person for a price and a job. It was apparent she had the right contacts, and used her brazen approach to bypass the long lines of waiting persons to achieve her objectives. Nothing was said. The entire arena was a full 180-degree change from what it used to be when there were so many milling around, like my grandfather, just waiting to get an acknowledgement or permission to enter the employment office. Because of the very high demands for labor, it seemed if you sought employment and passed a cursory review you were almost guaranteed employment.

CHAPTER 6
THE PROMISE TO FULFILL

It wasn't uncommon as one day's activity for five employment interviewers to process for hire between one to two hundred people. While I've tried to locate an actual copy of our daily requisition sheet I've been unsuccessful at this writing. For purposes of identification, that which was included on our work sheets was the department by name and number, the number of persons required for one day, and the rate designated for the identified job assignment. The rate of pay was shown at ten cents below actual, with understanding of a five-cent-per-hour increase at the end of thirty days, and the final nickel after sixty days of continuing employment.

The rate of the job was as quoted for an eight-hour day. Any adjustments from the rate for a day's work were by an across-the-board general increase or by overtime pay. The prerequisites for the job didn't involve an extensive interview, but rather a quick pass in conversation of what the applicant was seeking versus what was available on our daily requisition requirements. A quick examination of his application or past record and a go or no-go to the next station. Hundreds were being processed by the five employment representatives. Each job interviewer was given a copy of the requisition and filled the requirement for the jobs amongst the applicants coming in for placement. These were all hourly rated jobs and applicants. The salaried positions were, at least some of them, being handled at what was then our administration building, also located in the area. The interviewing for plant hourly work was far from a dignified interviewing approach, but simply an individual's response to basic questions, culminating in, "Can you work any shift?" and routing him or her to the next station. I wasn't as yet assigned to the hiring desk, but I was thoroughly acquainted with the job requirements. This assignment would be made only after I returned from the service. The place was a total madhouse with deals being made throughout the area. In one interesting situation during this period, I subsequently and innocently uncovered how a girl, at age thirteen, was placed on the employment rolls and carried this off for many years throughout the war years and for years after the termination of the war. I hope to recall to you later in the book how it occurred.

The entire Ford Rouge factory area was buzzing with wartime activity. People were being recruited from out of state for hire either in the Rouge facility with many government contracts or direct referral for placement at the new and large Willow Run bomber plant. This is where the B-24 Liberator bombers were being assembled and flight-tested. Wartime production was being done at most of the Rouge plant facilities as a consequence of converting the factory facilities from normal car or peacetime production to war-required products.

One of the main wartime buildings was the government-owned Rouge aircraft plant. This was the assembly and testing of the B-24 engines before being shipped to the Willow Run bomber plant. The bomber engine test cells ran the length of the building with creosote floor blocks to cushion the very heavy vibrations of the engine testing and loud noises. There were literally thousands of employees in this building alone, each working on their own requirement and each being paid by the hour at the very high Ford and government-elevated hourly rate. While all the people male and female alike worked on government-mandated assignments, there was also the occasion for stealing away secretly, for some fun time between males and females. Of the many situations and stories, most of which I care not to get into, there was one occasion that stood out and was very humorous to many. The mezzanine area used for storage and limited administrative offices was almost directly over the production assembly lines where the hourly employees worked. The setting provided a front-row-center arrangement for the workers to look up during work and watch an amorous escapade between a man and lady who thought they were well hidden. In reality, with the lighting behind and the drawn shades ahead, their actions were enlarged on the big screen, much to the amusement of many, simultaneously providing much laughter and amusement to the many below.

People were arriving in truckloads for employment, most of whom were recruited from the southern states, with little or no understanding of accommodations or, for that matter, money for their next meal. For all purposes it reminded me at the time of the motion picture I had seen, *The Grapes of Wrath*, but in reverse. The people were coming from all areas, out of state, and out of the country. There was work to be found and money to be made. The Rouge facility had in excess of eighty-five thousand employees, on a three-shift operation, not counting all the government people, foreign persons, and the thugs or cons just hanging around. This is compared to today's number ranging in size for the Rouge complex between six and eight thousand employees. People in the residential community were revamping their living quarters to accommodate extra paying tenants. The garages in the areas were converted into living quarters, many of which met all the standards of living and remained as convenient homes long after the war years. Everyone, it seemed at the time, was after that extra war dollar. Money was being made, big money.

It didn't take me long to fully understand who all these nondescript persons were within the office. They were, for the most part, assigned confidants of Mr. Ford's appointed overseer in the company, Mr. Harry Bennett, a man with a questionable background who gained the complete confidence of Mr. Ford and wheeled and dealed on the personnel issues as he saw fit. His power exceeded city mayors, police chiefs, and the like, all who were willing to respond

FORD TURNS 100

The Detroit Free Press
June 2, 2003

Bennett chapter a bizarre one

Thug, Ford's grandson sought clout

By SHERYL JAMES
FREE PRESS STAFF WRITER

It was Sept. 21, 1945 — the date of the famous executive shootout at the Ford Motor Co.

On one side of Henry Ford II's office at the company's Rouge complex in Dearborn was young Henry himself. He was 28, a tall man with a boxy build. Moments earlier, he had been voted president of his grandfather's company.

Facing him was Harry Bennett, 53, America's most-reviled corporate thug, the very stuff of wax museums. Head of the infamous Ford Service Department and for years a Rasputin-like confidant of an aging, ill Henry Ford, Bennett was vi-

cious and powerful and everyone knew it, including Henry II. It was an understatement to say the men disliked one another.

Ford eyed the short, stocky Bennett. Inside, he admitted later, he was flat-out scared of the guy. Bennett had good friends who were gangsters, several pet lions and a gun in his desk. Worse, he had everything to lose: Until that day, he believed old man Ford had fixed it so he would be president, not this spoiled Ford brat.

But that was before the Ford women got involved, and now — well, it was time for Henry II to rid the company of this cancer. He had to tread carefully.

From the collection of the Henry Ford

Henry Ford, left, visits Harry Bennett in Bennett's office. Bennett had gangster friends and several pet lions.

Detroit Free Press article (June 2, 2003)

FORD: An Era Remembered

to his dictates or suffer completely his strong arm of supreme authority. His function for all purposes was to control the people picture. He did this effectively by his strong-arm tactics. His hold on the company was through strengths both within the company and his control of the underworld. He was not identified with attempts to overpower the strengths and abilities of those running the manufacturing, production, and assembly processes of the company — these were not his domain — but rather exclusively those of Mr. Ford. The likes of executive personnel like Mr. Sorrenson, Mr. Roush, Mr. Jack Davis, and Mr. Bricker were but a few beyond the jurisdiction of Mr. Bennett.

Apart from the above, there were distinguished gentlemen standing around, and there were others, real thugs, with facial bruises, scarred and cut-up, and there were characters as one would see in the movies, with black sweaters and hats pulled down, as was their way of life. Hollywood would have benefited in a character study right within our office. These guys were tough, and apparently with sworn allegiance for duty on call from their benefactor Harry Bennett. I learned very quickly that I could learn from what I was experiencing, but had to work hard, no fooling around if I wanted to last, and particularly not to affiliate or get typed with one given group or another within the office. To alienate oneself by action or word of mouth in this unique society could easily be misread, frequently at one's own expense. I had occasion to see associates working in our midst one day, and the next day I would learn they were transferred to other locations or completely gone. The word was, you had a job, don't ask questions or interfere and you'd have the benefit of a paycheck and continuing employment. Tough surroundings, but real.

There was no such thing as security on the job. Your retention was based on what you did then and there— the slightest error was grounds for termination. In many cases, one didn't even have to err on the job. If someone took a disliking to another for whatever reason and felt that person was not wired to Mr. Bennett or Mr. Ford, he moved right in and got rid of the person, and by so doing created a vacancy for a friend or job-paying acquaintance. This was all attributed to Harry Bennett's henchmen's way of doing business, and the person affected had no recourse but to collect his final pay and get out. Conversely, through the dictates of Harry Bennett, a person could be taken off of a given assignment and placed in a position of supreme authority and responsibility without the slightest knowledge or understanding of the job. Several of these elite assignees I personally became acquainted with. I, like they, wondered where this unique and subconscious talent sprang from. It was not difficult to see, after being in these surroundings for a short time, the talent wasn't there, and it wasn't there from the beginning. This man, Harry Bennett, appointed by Mr. Ford and so well known within and outside the organization, made men quiver, and by a flick of his finger could cost an individual his job and income and care less for the person affected. Bennett's Napoleonistic demeanor was known by all as he ruled with the authority and dominance of an appointed king. Apart from his having defended Mr. Ford when he was being attacked in a fight many years before and subsequently being appointed by Mr. Ford as his confidant, the word was Harry Bennett, through his army, was the protector of the Ford family, particularly the grandchildren Henry II, Benson, William Clay, and their sister, Josephine. This was the period of much underworld activity — murders, kidnapping, speakeasies, and the like were common. This was the period of the Lindbergh kidnapping, which came to fall with considerable uncertainty on Bruno Richard Hauptmann. There were many then, as now, with a strong feeling the wrong man was convicted for this crime. In any event, there were no public overtures that the Ford kids were threatened, and this was always assumed to have been the result of Bennett's underworld knowledge and strengths. If any attempts had been made against the Ford family, the Bennett-established grapevine would have learned quickly of such developments and squelched such thinking quickly with strong repercussions following. Difficult to believe, but that nonetheless was the way it was.

This was a period of dynamic happenings and I had the opportunity to be there, all because of a promise I had made very early in life to get to the other side of the gate and help those who had no sponsors and needed assistance. I was allowed to enter into a different world and went along experiencing everything I was subjected to. Who would have thought this complete diversity existed?

Founder's granddaughter, philanthropist dies at 81

By Jenn Corney
FCN News Staff

Josephine Ford, the only granddaughter of company founder Henry Ford and one of the most significant philanthropists in metropolitan Detroit history, died June 1 at the age of 81.

Josephine (Dody) Ford

Ford, known as "Dody" to friends and family, provided unstinting financial support to arts, education, cultural and health care institutions in metropolitan Detroit. She also provided support for Acadia National Park in Maine, a state where she maintained a summer home. Throughout her lifetime she donated more than $155 million to organizations around the world.

She also became one of Ford Motor Company's largest shareholders, with more than 13 million shares of Class B stock (18 percent) at the time of her death. Those shares will remain in the hands of the Ford family.

Born in 1923 to Edsel and Eleanor Ford, she was the third of Henry and Clara Ford's four grandchildren. Ford married Walter Buhl Ford II, who came from another Ford family, and together they raised four children: Walter Buhl Ford III, Eleanor Clay Ford, Josephine Clay Ford and Alfred. Walter Buhl Ford II, a partner in the design firm Ford & Earl, died in 1991.

"Throughout her life, my aunt embodied the spirit of giving and family loyalty. She was an inspiration to all who knew her," said Chairman and CEO Bill Ford. "Her love for Ford Motor Company was unsurpassed and all of us will mourn her passing."

Article about death of Josephine Ford

CHAPTER 7
AN INTRODUCTION INTO THE FUTURE

Most of us were very proud of the positions we held and worked very hard to maintain the high standards we had set. There was no one setting out the parameters of responsibilities nor the accepted levels of proficiency. You assumed what the requirements of the job were and went about doing what you thought right. You, as such, made yourself the expert and people in the office came to recognize your talents and sought you out for answers. I knew I was right in my conclusions, particularly when my management came to me for detailed advice and recommendations.

I became more and more acquainted with the real strengths of those in the office, as well as those with assumed strengths. The politics and bluffing in the office, as well as the con artists, were all around and intermingled with the few who did the real work. The Bennett protégés were not too difficult to identify, nor were the persons looking out for their own well-being at the expense of the others. One learned a lot in this restricted and well-heeled society. By the same token, it was easy to alienate oneself by innocent word of mouth or actions. In a word, you had to be cautious and careful.

It was a difficult atmosphere to be associated with, but rewarding if one could survive. You were growing up mostly by listening and keeping your mouth shut. A hard lesson, but true.

We had very little freedom in the work area; suit and tie was the uniform of the day. No air conditioning, salt pill if one got dizzy, no breaks, and the men's room was the place if you wanted to get away for a minute, and the only place for a cigarette, if one smoked. The men's room was adjacent to the so-called bullpen area where hundreds of prospective applicants awaited their opportunity for an interview and hopefully job placement. This was where the long caravans of lunch wagons entered the facility and were dispatched to the office area and through the plant. The food was acceptable only, and a very far cry from the facilities that are available today.

Occasionally we pooled a ride within the office and rushed to the Dearborn area for lunch. It was difficult to have lunch and return within the thirty minutes allotted. However, when a supervisor accompanied you for lunch you could stretch the timing a bit. Captain's Diner was an excellent place for lunch once you had worked up on the three-deep lineup awaiting lunch. If one were to check out the location now, it still exists, however it was converted many years ago to a jewelry outlet.

Details of my meeting with Mr. A.J. Miller, formerly the personnel manager, at this location is reserved for still later identity in this book.

CHAPTER 8
THE ROUGE SLIP AND LARGE FREIGHTERS

Tom Silvester, office manager at the time, frequently asked me to join him for lunch. It was a good opportunity to review the happenings and plan for the next day's activity. We frequently went to a quaint, homespun Italian place on Fort Street, not far from the Ford Rouge facility, that had very good food. The location was in close proximity to the mooring area of the large ships coming and going, including the huge Ford ships and fleet, where they entered the Ford slip with their loads of iron ore, limestone, coal, sand, and the like. They came in for unloading or repairs as may have been needed, unloaded their cargo, and returned to the Great Lakes for their planned destinations and reloading. It was an on-going routine through the entire shipping season.

Now get the atmosphere—boats large and small coming and going, huge freighters being drawn into the Ford entryway, tugboats puffing and pulling as was their duty in aligning the freighters and attempting to maintain a clear entryway, the horns and whistles each calling for their individual attention, and the smell of fuel oil and crude all around as a part of the arena. You

Ford ships at dockside loading and unloading.

had to be there to appreciate the scene and to some limited extent enjoy what you were seeing.

There were several small bars along this waterway and adjacent to a large steel bridge which was operated by a man from an overhead cab. He responded to the on-coming ship traffic, opening the large bridge for their travel through and letting it down, holding up all street traffic. Little did I know that this may have been the baptism of fire for me, as in short order I would be given the unique assignment of maintaining the ships' complements at proper staffing levels. There seemed to be the typical ship-type persons roaming the area and the docks, awaiting work aboard one of the ships. This was the area where the eating place Tom Silvester knew about was located. Tom knew the proprietors well and by their greeting, they appreciated his acquaintance. They were at first somewhat hesitant in speaking openly as I hadn't been introduced, and based on their past problems, I could understand their sensitivity. Tom assured both husband and wife that my presence was as a friend and no relationship to any discomforts they may have had, past or present. Based on Tom's assurance to the owners, I was quickly accepted.

The owners confirmed, while we spoke, that Harry Bennett and his associates frequently had lunch in their restaurant, and at times they were requested to pre-pare special dinners for Bennett and friends. While he, Tom Silvester, had known Mr. Bennett and friends fre-quented the eating place, Tom said they never crossed paths. The point of this sidebar is to point out that the Italian owner had been threatened on more than one occasion by the underworld element and lived in con-stant fear for himself and his family, let alone his busi-ness establishment. This was due to his apparent failure to meet their demands which culminated in turn with threats to blow up his business establishment. This was the era of the strong Mafia dictates. The lady pointed out that the building had been wired with explosives, and failure to meet whatever the demands were would be reason to blow up the building. She obviously had the trust in Tom, and me now as well, to openly relay the story. It sounded at first far-fetched, until her husband proceeded to describe where the explosives and wires were located. As we left his place of business, he walked with us and proceeded to show us where the explosives had been removed, and where the wire had been cut and left dangling on the side of the building. This was done with no help from the local authorities of the crime-riddled downriver community. The owner had decided to tell Mr. Bennett, on one of his visits to the restaurant, of the threats, the sticks of explosives beneath his building, and also if he, the owner, failed to respond by a given day, the place would be reduced to rubble. The Bennett strengths and controls were well known, particularly in this the downriver community. The response the couple received was immediate and favorable. He assured them the situation would be fully taken care of, and there would be nothing to worry them further. Maybe he just liked the food. While they kept the restaurant open during the frightening several days that followed, it was not until they saw the same dangling wires that had been shown to us that their lives returned to some semblance of normalcy.

Our visits to this restaurant were at times followed with a trip to some of the well-kept residential areas in the downriver area. This was the same area Danny Thomas (Amos Jacobs) would come to entertain. His main club in this the Delray area was called Joey's Stables, a high-middle-class eating and bar establishment, not too far from our office location. I was with my boss and felt no guilt overstaying the normally considered lunch period. Our luncheon discussions were frequently intermingled with business and office subjects, making the office absence acceptable.

The homes and properties in the neighborhood were well maintained, and if the opportunity existed it would be wise, according to Tom, to buy several of the units, as family members were always willing to rent or lease in order to stay in their neighborhoods. He spoke of the coal cars on the sidings and how during the Depression the boys used to get coal for household use. His tones seemed to be reminiscing of his own youth, however never specifically identifying personal experiences.

This was not news to me as I too recall being hoisted into either the coal cars or the top of the ice cars, and throwing huge chunks of coal along the siding, in some instances while the cars were still slowly moving. Fred and Eddie, my uncles, with their big burlap sacks, would gather up the coal and put it in the wagons for transport back home. The ice experience was a little different, as it entailed getting into a small chute opening on top of the ice cars and pitching the ice over the top to the siding for pickup in anywhere from five- to twenty-five-pound chunks, all of which was left in the cars after unloading, whether coal or ice. When the weather was right we made many trips a day for coal, ending with enough to store for many days to come. With regard to the ice gathering, we would gather enough for two families to pack the iceboxes for several days ahead. No refrigerators for us, just the big icebox, requiring one to empty the big pail of water beneath as the ice melted.

These were all good experiences for me, which

allowed for better understanding of what it took to survive during these trying times. By the way, the loading onto the steel-wheeled wagon was the same wagon my grandfather and I used when we went to our favorite clover-cutting area, for food for our rabbits.

It's rather interesting to me and perhaps as a throwback to my association with Tom Silvester, that I ended up buying, remodeling, leasing out, or renting several comparable homes of the type we had seen. This was, in fact, a source of very good income for my purposes later in life.

Continuing on with the office activity, there was this neatly attired gentleman who positioned himself each day at the drinking fountain, obviously another Bennett appointee. Word had it, he owned or was affiliated with a car dealership, just south of the Ford Rouge area on Fort Street, or Jefferson. His drinking fountain position gave him direct visibility to the activity of the Ford hiring desk, the personnel coming through, and the offices both right and left and those exiting the premises. When someone wanted a drink, it was like moving a rock for him to step aside.

CHAPTER 9
THE INTRODUCTION OF GOVERNMENT PROGRAMS

It was during this period that specific government programs were being introduced into the office. There were no instruction manuals to follow, but rather this is what we need or what is required, and get it done. There were a couple of program concepts I was assigned to in the initial stages, one being the tire-rationing program for in-house employees.

After mulling around with several unworkable systems, I recall suggesting coordinating our efforts with the DSR, the Detroit Street Railway. They were the ones who had large tracking maps of the city and the far metropolitan areas. We needed this source information and could develop it further for our needs. It worked. We succeeded in getting these maps, and through a system of pinpointing each employee's main crossroads, we identified those interested in a "share the ride" program and aligned the employee with a specific route coming and going for others needing a ride. The system authorized new tires when needed for his vehicle, and anything less than participation in the program and Ford approval would not get him the needed tires. We covered two programs by this means: the tire program and the "share the ride" program. Both were determined to be highly successful and received the endorsement of the government and were adopted by other employers. While we had no manuals, journals, or otherwise to direct us, the Ford system was "get it done." Other programs were also underway such as "dollars for food" for those arriving without accommodations and needing seed money, housing referrals, and others. I was fortunate enough to have worked with, or basically assisted in establishing the structure of a given program and then moved by supervision to another assignment. The work was both challenging and rewarding as I got to know and understand the programs and then move on to other assignments and greater rewards.

One of the more memorable experiences happened to me during this period. At the time, I learned neither Mr. Ford nor Mr. Bennett had ever been in the employment office facilities. I couldn't understand this, as it was in my opinion the focal point of all things to come. It was their building, Mr. Ford's, and for them not to have seen or surveyed the facility was difficult for me to understand. This was where all the Ford people were hired or being processed in their employment requirements. This is where the salaried (at least most of them), the hourly, as well as the executive personnel were commencing, transferring, or being terminated. As I said before this was the area where the routing for the maker of kings began. By the same token, this was also where some of those who had gained fortune and fame were leaving per se, automatically out via the

Bennett fast-exiting alignment. I don't feel I'm over-emphasizing the situation nor am I rambling on too much about its importance. This analogy is and was as a result of my personal observations, understandings, and association of the facts, as well as other personal acquaintances, both within and outside of our office, and their understandings and appraisal of the events.

CHAPTER 10
MR. BENNETT WAS COMING

It wasn't long after I became fairly well acquainted with the requirement of the office and accustomed to the various daily stations that something strange happened. Word got around rather quickly, Mr. Bennett was coming to the office, for what reason I didn't know. Suddenly the place was void of managers, supervisors, and anyone who supposedly had authority, or a semblance of authority. They all left. They were fearful of being seen or being asked questions. The quickest way to avoid a possible confrontation at the time was to get lost. I have no way to describe to you the real fear that existed, other than to tell you all these self-made executives were all looking for a fail-safe hiding location. In the back area of the office building, I detected a lot of scurrying around and quite a lot of commotion. It was because Mr. Bennett had arrived. He was accompanied by four burly men, obviously his bodyguards, and his chief of plant security. He was a big one, an ex-athlete, who I believe was either from the University of Michigan or Michigan State University. Interestingly, there was no one to greet Mr. Bennett or his entourage or show him around. A strange setting. This surprised me to no end, but by the same token this scene supported my convictions. They reacted as best they knew how; they were afraid of a confrontation for whatever reason, and, as many before them, of losing their job. They had become acquainted with the consequences and their only defense seemed to be to avoid the possible contact with this assumed supreme little being, and thus protect their job and income.

I saw him from a not-too-distant vantage point, and couldn't help but think, "Why is everyone scurrying away from this little man with the bow tie?" He looked pretty much as I did, no extra arms or legs, however his attire was far from the type I would have selected. He was wearing a beige, extra-long, camel-hair coat for a man his size, about five foot seven. His little bow tie apparently was an offshoot of a fight he'd previously had protecting Mr. Ford. The tie was a change for him, resulting from someone trying to strangle him with his regular tie. The other thing that was obvious was his Al Capone wide-brim hat cocked on the side of his head. This Napoleonistic, small man apparently felt he was the cock of the roost (in this slice of society he was just that). I thought for but a second, and knew something had or should have been done by my superiors, nothing more than a courtesy acknowledgement. I took it up myself, "stupid," to handle the situation. There was no waiting for direction, as everyone of authority was in hiding or had left the building. I walked up to the oncoming cluster of rough-looking men with Mr. Bennett front and center. I startled both him and his associates, sort of catching him off guard. I introduced myself as a representative of the office, and if they wished I would assist. I wasn't about to extend my hand for a handshake, nor did I expect Mr. Bennett would either. His guards seemed somewhat uneasy by my effrontery and seemed to be awaiting his call as to what they should do with or about me. You customarily don't approach an individual of this type without an invitation or by direct order. Some may have thought my action to be senseless and on the brink of personal disaster. Others who had witnessed my innocent boldness were somewhat proud. The old-timers indicated my actions would be long remembered as no one before had ventured as far as I had without being swept aside by Mr. Bennett himself or his guards.

His dress, in my opinion, was in bad taste. He was an ex-sailor or merchant marine, a rough-and-tough street fighter, and didn't have much going for him as far as dress or style were concerned. To top it off as I approached him, I quickly observed he was wearing blue suede shoes, of all things. That did it, I had a personal good reputation for style and proper attire for both the office and after hours. This did it for me: I knew I was ahead of the game in dress and he had a long way to go. He obviously didn't respond to my courtesies, nor did I expect him to. All that was discernible was a slight half smile from this man indicating acknowledgement, and I stepped back. His bodyguards were uncertain of what actions they were to take as they pulled away from coming toward me. It could have been much worse, but I personally had concluded that he put his pants on as

I did, one leg at a time. There was no fear on my part in trying to be helpful, and if he or they felt otherwise, so be it. They proceeded in their travel as I stepped back. There were but a few clerks manning the records and hiring desk area as Mr. Bennett and his entourage swung around to the screening areas, entering what I had described as the bullpen area. The place was packed with people, some four to five hundred just waiting for their call to proceed. About this time there was loud shouting from Mr. Bennett's guard like hysteria coming into play, "Make way for Mr. Bennett, make way for Mr. Bennett." Like the parting of the seas for Moses, the aisle opened up, everyone stepped aside, not a word was said, and he and his guards passed through. It was something to behold. I doubt seriously if most of the people knew him, but most assuredly there were many in the midst of that carnage, pushing, and shoving, that had an insight if not understanding of the name and power. He swaggered by the crowd, with his hands in his back pockets, with his beige camel-haired coat pulled. His guards were ready to attack, while he appeared to revel in the authority, acting as though he was a Don or some supreme being entitled to such airs, as he went out the door to his waiting cars. He didn't meet with anyone, ask any questions, nor did he indicate interest in any particular thing. I was the only one that had anything to say to him. That was the end of it. He had come into the far side of the building, normally the exiting gate, walked the entire length, through the bullpen, and out. I thought many times if I could have had anything to do with his visit, as I had innocently commented more than once that neither he nor Mr. Ford ever visited the office. There were ears everywhere and quite possibly, through one of his many henchmen, the word had gotten to him. It was just too coincidental that I had been mentioning this lapse of good management practice, that he should suddenly out of nowhere and for no known reason come to our facility. You be the judge of this. On the other hand, his strong henchmen were on the payroll and everywhere in our building and quite possibly through their services and lines of *sotto manne* communications, there was no need for him or Mr. Ford to come to the building. As I'm certain, he was kept informed and knew exactly what was going on.

Apart from being involved in the special war jobs that came into being during this period, my assignment was basically to audit the hiring forms of the newly hired or rehired employees. If the employee had not signed up for the insurance program, we were required to seek out why, and try to get them to accept. The interesting point was that we had a representative of the insurance company in our midst. If we failed in our attempts, he took up the responsibility and generally achieved a successful conclusion. It was strange, but true, that I was being told to do the work for the insurance company—just another facet that I didn't understand amongst the many in the office. This didn't mean that much to me, since the insurance representative was a very gracious individual, always with a fresh flower for the girls in the office and a kind word to the men. Whether he was, in fact, a bona fide insurance representative or just another con working for an in-house party, I'll never know. Nor for that matter, his activities other than being a representative of the insurance company and being diligently on the job each day, never became truly suspect.

Every so often there seemed to be an individual who couldn't be swayed toward accepting the company insurance programs. In short order, it was again obvious, the con men were at it again. The way they were working was based on a promise the interviewer at the hiring desk (the con) had made to the newly processed employee. He had all the pertinent information on the individual, including home address, marital status, and the names of his whole family. "I'll come to see you at your home in a day or two, and we'll discuss an insurance package for you at that time," is the way the word was given, and secretly. In the meantime, the new employee was being told, don't sign up for any other insurance coverage as that may serve to disqualify you from a program I'll have in your name. This was the way the con was introduced — the new employee was steadfast in his refusal during forms processing. He had established a friend for his supposed security for the future, and meanwhile, little did he know, he subjected himself to a long-term insurance package for himself and more often for his entire family and relatives. The employee felt he had bypassed the system and had gained a friend or a "drag" with an important Ford executive, protecting his employment for the future. The selling con artist declined to consider the company's interests and made happen that which was profitable for himself on a continuing and long-range return basis. In the meantime, once hooked, the employee made payment for himself and as many family members as he could be talked into well into the future.

CHAPTER 11
THE CON GAMES CONTINUE

While the insurance con game was flourishing, management didn't stop the practice even though, in my opinion, they seemed to be aware of it. The practice gave rise that perhaps more than one person was involved and payoffs were being made along the line. Those of us who had our suspicions of the activity and absent of involvement or proof chose to remain silent, as we did not have the full perspective of the action, and our finger-pointing or accusing would have possibly led to our own demise. Our attitude was that those involved would eventually overplay their hand and get caught. In fact, I was within earshot when the culprit involved was being told by Tom Silvester, office manager, to desist in the practice and failing would result in dismissal. He never did change his habits for as long as I knew him and challenged his management to take whatever actions they wished. He was, in fact, making too much money, and it wasn't feasible for him to be let go. While other actions could have been taken, like reassignment to a different job, this didn't occur. Our convictions that management was aware were nevertheless confirmed. It was their call, not mine. The insurance con practice in Ford, and the selling con in this instance were terminated, however the insurance practice flourished as a non-Ford entity on the outside, and to this day to my knowledge, continues to exist independent of Ford.

Another bold game was going on in the bullpen area. This is where the applicants were being corralled into the various lines awaiting interviews for a job, or were turned away. Those falling short of passing into the positive lineups were conveniently taken aside, knowing well they were heading toward the exits, and asked to further discuss their interests. It was obvious that he was vulnerable—he was seeking a job and had just been turned away. Quietly and not based on any qualifications, he was asked if he'd be willing to purchase a new car as his token of sincerity and to keep the transaction quiet, in exchange for a job. The answer was most assuredly yes and the beat moved on. Many cars were sold in this fashion with the con man collecting commissions on each sale and again at the expense of the employment practices and benefiting the con guy in the bullpen area, and the Lincoln-Mercury dealer who at the time was located in the Dearborn area, not too far from the main office of the company at 3000 Schaefer Road.

While there were many more little favors being exchanged for jobs, there was also the jobs and money being exchanged at the grocery store in South Dearborn. The guards at the gate effectively delivered on their job promises and were obviously wired to one of the job interviewers or management, who frequently directed interviewers to hire a given applicant. Another was the young lady I previously spoke of, who would make a periodic visit to our office never wanting to stop to talk to any other than a specific interviewer and always with a different man she had recruited and was directing for employment. I've but covered just a few scams and the related details how the job and money or other benefits were exchanged. There were other money-making schemes, but we'll set these aside for another time.

CHAPTER 12
PEOPLE AND PROGRAM CHANGES

There were many celebrities working for Ford during this period. I had the opportunity to become acquainted with many of them and, in fact, we worked together on a number of projects. One was Jack Jawar of golfing fame. He spent much of his free time showing us the correct swing of golf and generally the ethics of the game. Others included Norm Smith, of hockey fame, while Rollie Rolston, also of hockey fame, frequently came into the office and was at the time a supervisor in one of the Ford facilities and a supervisor of my brother-in-law, Gene. Also in our midst was a wrestler, whose name as I recall was Johnny Silva. His strengths were displayed by his ability to literally tear a phonebook in two. It was something to behold as the beads of sweat rolled off his brow, and his fine silk shirt was pulled apart by the muscular action and energy to accomplish this feat. This was all done for a small audience who would congregate in the men's room for a smoke break. Smoking was not permitted elsewhere in the office area. The other big names that worked with us were Jesse Owens of track fame, and big Jim Thorpe who eventually got the recognition he deserved. We'll talk more about these last two later in the book.

I became personally acquainted with Tommy Bridges, the baseball player of the Detroit Tiger organization, during this period. As an early enthusiast and an avid follower of the game as far back as 1933, I felt particularly proud to be in the company of this locally renowned strong right-handed curveball hero. Tommy was a quiet, unassuming guy, easy to talk to and recognized by most. The Detroit fans were highly appreciative of his strong performances as a Tiger, in that they presented him with a new Cadillac during his tenure. He was good enough to recognize my transportation to and from work by public transportation, and as a consequence he would frequently stop to pick me up or return me in the vicinity of home at day's end. It was something to behold as we were waved through the main gate by the guards, driving in with this brand new Cadillac in the strong midst of Ford country.

Tommy, like many other name persons, was given assignment within the office areas of the company during his off-season availability. His basic area of assignment was the newly created labor relations area, located on the second floor of the employment building. Tommy's credentials for the assignment appeared to be nothing more than those of an observer. He sat at a main table, surrounded by many company and union people. Jack Blott was the lead company guy, formerly the University of Michigan line coach. The big, dominant-looking individual didn't seem to say much, but on the other hand he acknowledged my presence when I had occasion to be in his office area, and I was treated respectfully.

Copy of agreement between Ford and union

This was a short period after the UAW came into being at Ford. All contractual requirements between the parties were by hit and miss, as no one fully understood the positions they were to take. Jack Blott created a labor relations team with associated company representatives, mostly from Ann Arbor. These included an attorney from an Ann Arbor law firm, an associate who was said to have been the organ teacher of Harry Bennett's daughter, and a man who had a cleaning establishment in Ann Arbor before or during the time he was with Ford. Also included was Henry Aquinto of North Packard, Ann Arbor, and a stenographer whose name I believe was Bob White. Tommy sat with the group, while on the side opposite was the union's representation. This included Paul St. Marie, the first president of the Union Local 600. I don't believe they had a union meeting hall at the time as their facilities in the south end of Dearborn came into play much later. Percy Lewellan, their vice president, was there as were others including those representing individuals being directed to this body for discipline. The line of persons awaiting disciplinary action extended from the second floor down the stairwell of the building out the door and adjacent to the lineups of people seeking employment. That made for an odd mix entering the building.

It was interesting to observe. Someone would read aloud the charge or infraction (I believe it was Bob White, the male stenographer), then Mr. Blott, the Ford lead man, would mumble something, and on to the next man they would go. If the employee was given time off the job as a penalty, Bob White would initiate action to withhold his clock card until the penalty imposed was served and arranged for the card release on a specified date. For the most part, the union accepted the company's recommendations and only in rare cases would they raise a complaint. This was the beginning of what was to become the labor relations department of Ford. Its modus operandi was by trial and error and through this system grew into a science for the many who were to follow both in management and union. Tommy Bridges sat and merely observed the activity as an interested party.

Party factions were becoming openly apparent, and loyalties were also surfacing. Jack Blott, as the appointed labor relations director of the company, appeared to be acting quite independently of the employment director, Mr. A.J. Miller (the gentleman I spoke of having met at the restaurant earlier). The initial labor relations between the company and union, as a consequence of the first contract dictates, appeared to be nothing more than a disciplinary body by the company, while the union hierarchy sat in attendance observing the action taken. On occasion, if the union representative hearing the case felt the penalty to be too severe, or if they felt the actions improper, particularly if the disciplinary action was against a friend or associate, the union was known to defend the individual seeking relief for their political well-being. The lineup of those awaiting discipline, as I said before, was so long that it went from the office down the adjoining stairwell out the gate and adjacent to those awaiting entry into the building for job interviews and placement. The charges being read in this labor relations arena were more often than not being away from the job, excessive scrap, loafing, etc. This became so repetitious that it became monotonous, as were the penalties: one day off, three days off, or even discharge. These were the initial steps of a highly important decentralized labor relations function throughout the entire company. Tommy Bridges, like the many other boys of summer who were fortunate enough to get summer employment at Ford, just waiting around for their opening day, was merely an observer.

The word had gotten around that Jack Blott had no obligation to the employment director, A.J. Miller, who was still on the executive payroll responsible for the Ford personnel office. The fencing for authority and power created quite a strain on those normally recognizing a straight-line organization. The dual and independent reporting configuration left some major questions in the reporting relations. This resentful relationship was carried to the point of Mr. Blott refusing to accept his salary from Mr. Miller, asking that it be returned to the sender. This was an overt and obvious statement, indicating disregard to the past strongly accepted practices, identifying Mr. Miller as the main authority within the employment office. Keep in mind this is the same man I spoke of that I'm sure I had seen at Captain Johnson's eatery. The exercise in strengths went on for a long period of time, without announcement of a change of the guard or the authority to those of us trying to keep the office activity in good handling. While we surmised the direction was coming into play from much higher levels, the Harry Bennett stronghold versus that of Mr. Bugas, now of the Ford block, it was all beyond our specific understanding and, therefore, until told to change our habits or being told we were removed from the payroll, we just kept on going. The real work continued as before, and we kept the employment activity moving. The uncertainty of our well-being, particularly those of us who like myself had no allegiance other than to an honest day's work, was stressful. Others, who were on the bubble of uncertainty and watching the infighting, continued with their daily activity. Included was Willis Ward, the football great who ultimately became a successful attorney after leaving Ford and eventually became a highly regarded judge in the state. It was quite interesting to watch Willis Ward practicing for his bar examination early each morning. His deep, bellowing voice echoed up and down the aisle ways while he rehearsed his arguments for or against his imaginary clients. Others in this same office area, referred to as the Ford sociological department, included Mrs. Meggs, who seemed to have responsibility for resolving the female problems within the working environment. Another individual was Jack Sharkey's fight promoter, or a fighter of that caliber who was believed to respond directly to Mr. Bennett. He subsequently laid fame to the comment to Mr. Bennett, "What are we to do with Abbie the Bish?" Mr. Abblewhite had been the head of a small northern

Michigan congregation, and was being referred to as the Bishop. Like many of the time, Mr. Abblewhite was hired directly by Mr. Ford and given the responsibility of the sociological department. Bennett was sought by a protégé before accepting direction from a non-Bennett office assignee. The backgrounds of some of my associates during this era were complete stories unto themselves. I'll not attempt detailing with this writing but will leave such for perhaps subsequent consideration. It became commonplace for me in the office to be frequently queried as to who my mentor was, seeking to uncover my status versus their own. My response was I got my job as they did. I was tested, qualified, and was assigned to the employment activity. This was the truth. It was apparent that those bold enough to come right out and ask the question were uncertain of their own well-being. Not many of them believed me, particularly as from my perch directly overhead, I had hung a picture of Mr. Ford. Some claimed I resembled Mr. Ford and that there was a likeness in our looks. I let stand their individual thoughts and went about my business. They left perplexed and frequently mentally self-assured that I hadn't given them the whole truth, and that I was in fact an associate of the Ford family. Coincidentally, we did eventually have a niece or other direct relative of Mr. Ford also working within the sociological department, and I, in the minds of many, to satisfy their own inhibited curiosities, must have also fallen into this Ford family category. Good enough for me.

As I've said before, most of us were very proud of

Do you think we looked alike? Nonsense. By the way,
my picture appears elsewhere in this story.

the positions we held and worked diligently to maintain the high standards we had set out for ourselves. There was no setting out of the parameters of responsibility because there were none. You assumed what you felt to be the accepted levels of proficiency required for the particular function and did your work accordingly. You made yourself the expert and people, both before your assignment and after, came to recognize you as the expert and in turn, as I said earlier, called on you for assistance and advice. You knew you were doing the right thing particularly when management came to you for detailed information and recommendations. At this time, I was only nineteen years of age playing the role of a fully knowledgeable and mature person and accepted in this role.

I became more and more acquainted with the real strengths of those within the office, as well as those with assumed strengths. The bluffers and the con artists were all still around and unfortunately intermingled with the few who understood the work requirements of the office. Harry Bennett's protégés were not difficult to identify, nor were those merely looking out for their own well-being, frequently at the expense of others. I was able to learn a lot in this restricted and well-heeled society. You had to keep your mouth shut and do your job. Any inferences relative to cliques or groups could and would easily be interpreted improperly and be detrimental to one's employment status.

We had very little freedom in the office work area; suit and tie were the uniform of the day. No air conditioning, salt tablets, the men's room the only location if you got sick or wanted to break away for a while. In that we were located adjacent to the eight famous Ford smokestacks on one side, and the Ford coke ovens on the other, our office area was the receptacle to a heavy array of fallout: soot, smoke, and toxic foundry odors. The clean and heavily starched shirts didn't last long in this setting, and were visibly dirty by day's end.

CHAPTER 13
THE ALIEN REGISTRATION PROGRAM

It was about this time, early 1943, that I was assigned to the alien registration activity. This like many others was a unit within the employment activity, however under the jurisdiction of the labor relations department. This, as it came to pass, was one of the more interesting assignments I had been given. The work revolved around a government edict that each person working in a government-contract activity, as the Ford Motor Company was, had to be cleared by Washington to remain working. All aliens—i.e., persons without United States citizenship status—had to be brought into the alien registration department, which had been set up for this purpose. They were interviewed, requiring responses to detailed questions, identifying specifically where they had worked since entering the United States, exact dates and names of places, and then they were cleared by the government before being given the opportunity to remain.

As previously indicated, we had in excess of eighty-five thousand people within the Rouge complex, with additional non-company employees who also had to be verified as U.S. citizens. The responsibility was detailed and complex. The requirements were handled in concert with the Fifth Service Command of the Army which at that time was centrally located in the old Graham-Paige factory. They, too, had hundreds of government people working for them. Our job was to coordinate and process through them the completed government forms, which we had completed on behalf of the person seeking work in the contract unit, or those who would in fact be removed from the job and held in abeyance pending government approval. They, the Fifth Service Command, would either pass on the application in the first instance or reject it. From there, the materials were forwarded to Washington, who did the same. If the applicant was acceptable, Washington returned the approving affidavits to our office for coordination with the employee and authorization for work or return to work. The entire process took two to three weeks for final clearances. The applicant was off the job until clearance had been given. Those awaiting employment, whether from Canada, Poland, Italy, Germany, etc., would be on standby awaiting their Washington clearance. Once we received the required documentation, usually in a week or two, we'd contact the employee involved and coordinate his return to the job. The non-employee was sent for, via registered mail, and given the good news that he had passed the requirements and a job offer was imminent. All company records had to be checked against citizenship status, the employee had to be located in the facility he or she was working, arrangements had to be made to allow for a replacement, and then they were required to appear in our office for their required government approval processing. This meant thousands upon thousands of recorded alien personnel within the Rouge facility were required to submit to this requirement or be turned away from their employment on the Ford government contracts. This edict for clearance, by the government to my knowledge, dealt only with those employers who in fact had received war contracts as Ford had. Others, I believe, were exempted from this requirement.

My responsibilities were those of basically a high-powered clerk. I knew how to work with people, overseeing the responsibilities, and with some eight young female assistants as a typing pool, handling the heavy typing workload requirements, and above all, keeping the workflow moving. As I remember, they had no idea of my age, and their suggestive jokes, which I didn't truthfully understand, just kept flying over my head, while I was shying away from temptation and keeping my mouth shut. I reported to an elderly gentleman who sat directly across from me at a two-sided desk, with a phone on swivel arrangement between us. If the call was for Johnny I merely swung the swivel holder his way for his response or vice versa if the call was for me. This is the way things were done at that time. Johnny kept his head down, a continuing carryover of the Bennett syndrome—don't get in the way or find yourself responsible for answers. He was my friend, proud and appreciative of his job, however lacking in the attributes needed to fulfill all of the related job requirements. He was one who repeatedly cautioned me to avoid contact or conflict, as one never knew whose toes or clique you were treading on. This was the way it was, and by today's way of doing business it seems awkward and cumbersome. When I worked for Johnny, he had it down to a science — always check over your shoulder to make sure no one was observing or overheard what was being said and in this way ensure you had a job to return to the next day. In fact, many of his responses were simply a nod of the head, or no answer at all. You had to get to know him to understand him. He wasn't much different than many others from within, who had adopted their own unique way of staying out of the way and still being assigned a job. A good example of what I mean was the stuttering. There were more than a few who, by design or subconsciously, seemed to resort to stuttering in communicating. The oddity was that in friendly conversation the stuttering wasn't there. The name that came into play at the time was that they were afflicted with "Forditis" as a consequence of being around for a long period and put into the position of having to respond to many situations when asked to do so, and not having an immediate answer. Johnny had, as I recall, confidence in my efforts in the office, and frequently let me improve on the requirements and at times introduce new concepts into what we were doing, making for a smoother transition from one phrase to another in our job content. Johnny, like many, however, had the scare built into him — he wouldn't try anything different for fear of being challenged and criticized. Like many others of the time, he was an ex-athlete, having gained fame in the boxing ring. He related to me how he got his start while overseas with the Canadian Army. It began with a three-day pass, the prize in his battalion for anyone winning a match in their weight class. Anxious to see the big city and break away from the mundane daily life of an army private, he volunteered, and got severely beaten, but began a boxing career from that introduction. Johnny, years later, became the welterweight champion of Canada. Like many other athletes in bygone years, he too ended up on the Ford payroll. Johnny was a rough-looking dude with a cauliflowered ear, as though he had been a wrestler rather than a boxer. He had very heavy upper-body strength, was round-shouldered, and built like a tank. I remember him well, as he more often than not cornered me in the office on the pretence he was reliving his boxing days—first blows to the head, then to the midsection, then back to the head. Thankfully he was only going through the motions without packing a punch. If he had decided to use his real boxing skills, he would have flattened me with his first blow. Johnny and I had many fun moments, however never inter-rupting our work priorities nor jeopardizing our work requirements.

I've described Johnny in some detail, however, there's much more. For one thing he was very neat in his attire, usually a gray suit and a light-gray shirt and matching tie. Always clean shaven and his graying, well-groomed hair appearing as though he had just left the barber. That which struck me as interesting was to see a rough and tumble individual wearing modern-looking glasses typing with one finger, and with nails polished. Johnny was well-groomed, which dissuaded one from concluding he was a pug. He obviously didn't want or like such inferences and conducted himself with all the social graces he could muster.

While not many were aware of Johnny's background and boxing interests, it was apparent to me, particularly as many of his young boxer acquaintances and understudies would appear in the office to say "hello" to him, or to await a referral for employment. One of the local boxers was Adam Pianga, known in boxing circles as "Young Kid McCoy." He was one of the youngsters Johnny had been training and who became a recognized winner during the time Johnny managed him. Johnny was still in the fight game and enjoyed the relationships he had developed in the past, however, not allowing his past interests to surface or conflict with his primary source of income: his job at Ford. Johnny was my friend.

Our office was directly across the aisle from what was to become the company's beginnings of labor relations. This is the area where Jack Blott and the Ford negotiating team sat around the big table with the union. Again Tommy Bridges sat with the group. Frequently I glanced out the door to observe what was going on and more often than not I'd catch Tommy's eye and by a shrug of his shoulders, he let me know he didn't know what was going on and wished he was someplace a million miles away. We laughed it off many times. The other most interesting happening was within our office.

While I've already described the basics, there was still another major point of concern—we had a third occupant in the relatively small office area that Johnny and I occupied. For purposes of this story we'll call him Mike, as that name appropriately suits him. Mike was just another Bennett trustee who used the chair in our office as his command post. Talk about a rough-looking character—he was definitely on the top of that list. Black sweater, matching black hat, shabby dark trousers and, in effect, all in black. He was usually asleep or dozing off in the corner and making it difficult to carry on a conversation with an applicant or for that matter across the desk. Neither Johnny nor I understood his role but suffice it to say he wasn't reporting to the same supervision that we were aligned with. It became apparent that his instructions were being communicated to him via our office and the phone Johnny and I used on the swivel. When the phone rang I would answer assuming it was for either Johnny or me, but on occasion, about two or three times a week, it was for the clown Mike who sat in the corner. The caller wouldn't identify himself, but merely asked to speak to Mike. I'd give Mike a nudge, and he'd pull his hat back and answer the phone. The conversation was nothing more than, "Yeah, all right, yeah," and he'd leave. I would look over at Johnny, half questioning what was going on, or what was to happen, and I soon learned he didn't know any more than I did and chose to ignore the situation, pretending it wasn't happening.

It became apparent Mike's calls were coming to him from Harry Bennett himself or one of his aides. The trouble situation would be identified and Mike was the hammer. He apparently did his job, returned to our office looking beat-up, the blood stains on his hands and clothing giving him away. I never asked and he never told. Johnny just put his head down or looked the other way as if he hadn't heard from the side of his cauliflower ear. That's the way it was, and the office routine just went on.

For some unknown reason, big Mike took a liking to me, and when he'd come back from wherever it was he had been directed to, he would toss a knife or a gun across my desk, and with a cock-eyed smile say, "Here, put this one in your collection." I don't know how I got away with my comments to this gorilla, but I vividly recall telling him I would beat the hell out of him if he didn't shape up. I would say, "Don't come back to this office until you're washed up or I'll throw you out on your ear." Sometimes he would laugh, but more often than not, he would wash the blood from his hands, clean himself up, and then return to his favorite lounging chair in the office. Here I was, tall and thin, weighing about one-fifty, facing off with this rock, built like a refrigerator, who could have had me rolling down the stairwell next to our office with just one swipe of his muscular hands and arms. Not many people talked to Mike and for some reason or other he got a particular kick out of my comments to him. I was glad Mike responded to me and my comments as he did. Absent a sense of humor between us, this setting could have led to an impossible situation for me. Mike looked at me as a friend, I don't know why, and I was glad to leave it at that.

Either Johnny or I would do the interviewing of the candidates for government permit authorizations, and at times we would not only come across most interesting people's backgrounds, but uncover a situation which, for all other purposes, had been best left unsaid. The forms calling for responses were long and detailed. There were eight sheets measuring eight-and-one-half by sixteen with exacting information requirements. Failure to comply in responding to the information requested unfortunately nullified the entire process. It was particularly interesting when it came to questioning female applicants as to their source of income over a given period. After a while I got to recognizing their reasons for not divulging their income, and had to assist by indicating prostitution was an acceptable answer, and it usually was the answer. In other instances the applicant would choose to reject further response because of fear that his or her prior income, or activities per se, such as being incarcerated, would be fair game for others. Often, to assure the applicant the information given was confidential, I would postpone the interview until he or she was better prepared and ask that they jot down all the specific dates and places of employment or periods of income and we would try once again. I remember well my particular experience with Mr. Kenney, who fortunately gave me a delay of time to get my personal credentials in order before disqualifying me for a job. This was the least I could have done for an individual needing the job, and because of some past indiscretion on their part, coming close to being rejected. What was most satisfying to me was that after counseling them through their dilemma, most were assured that the direction I had given was proper, and together we succeeded in getting them their government approvals. While there was the necessary reject from time to time, I felt I had done all I could to do right by the individual and felt confident that I had.

There are many more situations that come to mind now that I'm relaying some of my experiences during this era. To try recalling more than several would be, to some, mere storytelling without real substance. Therefore, I'll restrict myself to the situations where, hopefully, the reader of this factual portrayal of life inside Ford will accept this writing as the truth, and better comprehend what the difficulties for many were then, as opposed to now. Should other situations come to mind that I have not included it may be necessary to include them in still other publications to shed greater light on the trials and tribulations during this era.

Keep in mind the disparity of those seeking the opportunity to work in a war production effort. They were coming in from all walks of life and literally from all parts of the country. They needed work, and they needed money to feed their families. Also intermingled with the new applicants were those already working who had to be removed from their employment and income pending government clearance. The wages were excellent and the job opportunity fell in line as one's patriotic duty to participate. It was very trying for some to recall life's events, employers, and income sources over an extended period of years. Once finalized, all original signatures on the forms were required before forwarding to the typists for final original copies. We usually kept ahead of the typing pool by eight to ten handwritten and completed forms. They in turn had to type each sheet as an original and designate its routing. There were eight sheets to a completed package. By today's standards, using a computer would have been a blessing.

I specifically recall that one of the application forms either Johnny or I filled out was missing an original signature. This was a relatively young lady from Canada with all the credentials for job acceptance and placement. Her residence was listed in the Dearborn area and not too distant from the office. This omission created in Johnny's mind a major problem, as it necessitated mailing a registered receipt letter asking the applicant to return for signature. Anything less would make the requesting application form improper and void. A situation I felt could be easily remedied represented to Johnny an insurmountable and bold venture. I merely suggested to Johnny that I'd handle the situation without fuss or bother. I'd get a company car, go to the residence of the applicant, get the signature, and return. Unfortunately, there was no phone number listed on the application, or it could have been handled by calling her and having her return to the office. While my approach was logical, it was unique and basically unheard of, as there were too many possibilities of error or at least question, at least according to Johnny. The logic was on my side, while Johnny tried to dissuade me. I convinced him I'd get the use of the one company car we had for the entire office, from my former supervisor Tom Silvester, get the signature, and return. I finally got him to sign the request form, assuring all would be well. Johnny was so upset that he just paced the office area while I proceeded to go to Tom Silvester for his approval. He looked at the request and merely said, "Oh," signed it, and told me to be careful. Apparently Tom, like Johnny, was surprised, and acted with guarded optimism. Johnny was pleased with the endorsement, and let the situation surface and pass as his recommended handling. This whole situation represented a new way of administration for both and in a way they were happy to participate.

As I had said, the address of the applicant was a short distance from the office, three to five miles at the most, and wouldn't take me long to get there and back. I left at about 9:30 a.m., was pleasantly greeted upon arriving, immediately recognized, and asked to enter. While I proceeded with an explanation of my visit, I didn't get very far and was asked to wait to meet the family. I expected to meet her husband and kids. I waited an abnormal period of time and no one showed up. About then I was told the coffee would be done shortly, and much to my surprise two lovely young ladies came into the room, still somewhat asleep, as the mother scurried about trying to convince me to stay for a while. Keep in mind, I was young while mature in my mannerisms. I, like most of my generation, was not accustomed to the proposition of being the one served up by the mother on behalf of the daughters. There was no father around nor any comment relative to others in the family. That which the mother spoke of was that both daughters had come to the United States with her and hadn't found employment. Again it was obvious as to what she sought. Quick comparisons, then versus now, would have one conclude my actions were less than believable, however it should be understood that the times dictated precautions, and any overt actions on my part to the contrary could have been the ruination of a career, let alone a total collapse of the confidence that had been extended to me by both Tom Silvester and Johnny McIntyre. The purpose of relaying this experience was again to emphasize the disparity of the times for many, and the idea of anything for a job, including putting up the daughters as bait for possible employment.

I finally got the signature, practically tearing myself away from the mother of the household, assuring her all would be done to expedite approvals, and she would be notified accordingly. I was not in a position to accept favors from, or to offer employment to, her young daughters. My rejection of the sub rosa offers was not understood, and almost appeared surprising to her. By today's standards there are many who would conclude I was a damn fool for bypassing the invitation. That was then and this is now.

Many situations that arose during this period could have led to a complete disaster for me personally and for the objectives I had set much earlier for myself. As a side there were those who threw all caution to the wind and were ultimately caught in their foolhardy acts, losing reputation, job, and their employment. Ask me sometime about the government guy assigned to work with us who got too friendly with one of our very lovely nineteen- or twenty-year-old girls in the records storage area. Both were summarily dismissed. In this case between the mother and daughters, they would have gladly sacrificed themselves for a job at Ford. The bottom line was, her approval did finally come through and she did get a job at Ford. I never did learn what became of her daughters or who they attempted to gain their favors from next.

Quickly, and almost on the heels of the experience with the lady from Canada, I was interviewing a salaried referral from within the company who was reported as an alien and not authorized to work without the proper clearances. Surprising to me was that he was working in our photographic laboratories, a highly restricted and confidential work area. His name has stuck with me over the years and I've often wondered what his relationship was to the United States government. His last name was (I believe) Von Monshenheim, and I couldn't have thought of a better name that automatically conjured thoughts of spy work or at least fifth-column activities, and this man ideally fit the image. The name to fit his last name must have been Baron. He was a perfect gentleman in our meeting, spoke with a slight German accent, and was tall and erect and immaculate in his exacting attire. I couldn't understand how it was that an individual such as this was working in our photographic laboratories, where all the gun-site photographs were on file for the B-24 bombers, where all the top-secret photographic data was being developed, where all of the top-secret prints of all the Ford government data was available, and above all where no persons were authorized to venture. Baron Von Monshenheim was right in the middle of all this and we were at war with his country, our worst enemy. Strange, but that's the way it was, and here I was thinking that I had to go into the service before long against his country. This was just another thing that I couldn't understand within my experiences of growing up in an arena of many happenings.

I asked the required questions, as I would with any other applicant, and he responded dutifully. He informed me of his place of birth, his educational background, where he had been and was employed. He described his current duties and continued in our session that his presence and confidential work activity in our photographic department was not as alarming as some might think. I for one couldn't accept this rationale, but I had no say in the matter and continued doing my assignment. Now here's the kicker. When we completed all the required administrative details, all signed and awaiting the typist's handling, he courteously asked if he could be so bold as to ask where the routing of the materials would be, after final typing, and what activity within the War Department in Washington would issue the final authorization. I recall showing him a sample clearance certificate and accompanying authorization card which were issued, once cleared for work in a government-approved facility such as Ford. I thought it odd that he sought the specific details. I informed him that his clearance would take two to three weeks, and once received I would contact him and present him with the proper War Department clearance.

To my surprise, he said that he would go to Washington immediately and return with the needed document. I tried to tell him of our normal forwarding via the Service Command at the old Graham-Paige plant, but this didn't seem to faze him. He thanked me, stood tall and erect, whirled around, and left. I felt I had done all I could and if he chose to go to Washington, it was his call. All I knew was here's a man in our employ who looked as though he belonged to the German Command, an employee who had greater access to the top war secrets of the company, and the United States of America for that matter, than I would ever hope to have, and no one seemed to sense the urgency or concern. Just another thing within the Ford Motor Company, happening right before me, and I was to do nothing, and didn't.

Within four days from the time Baron left my office, he returned. He asked to see me and I assumed perhaps he had more questions. I couldn't have been further from the point in question. He came in, handed me an envelope with my name on it, stood at what was strict attention, again as one would expect a German officer's actions to be. To my surprise he had the clearance needed signed by the general's staff of the War Department, and that was it. I thanked him, directed him what to do next, returning to him the wallet-sized approval identification card, and that ended our relationship. I didn't ask nor did he respond with further information. Interestingly enough he was one of several hundred that I had a hand in assisting in this effort, and any time I went to our main office, the location that housed the company's main photographic laboratories, I would see him and the thought ran through my mind, "What side is he really on?" Our winning the war gave testimony, thank God, to the fact that he must have been on ours.

CHAPTER 14
MILITARY SERVICE AND OUT

It wasn't very long after my assignment in the alien registration activity of the Ford Motor Company that I was heading for the service. My first consideration at the time was to enlist in the United States Air Corps. I prepared for and passed the enlistment tests and bid my family and friends goodbye. Unfortunately, I went through an exercise of futility, as after being introduced into the Air Corps and sent to their initial staging area, the enlistment, for whatever reasons, was cancelled. I was told that their quotas for the states of Michigan, Ohio, and Indiana had been filled. The entire contingency was routed back to their home depot and told to report to their respective boards for instructions. This action delayed my induction into the army by several months.

Fortunately, except for my basic training, my army experience for the most part paralleled the type of work I had been doing in civilian life. Based on my administrative aptitude, including once again my typing speed, I was assigned, following basic training, to headquarters. For approximately the next three years I was assigned to the enlisted men and officer orders section in charge of the office, with responsibility for the processing of personnel, both in and out of the replacement center, numbering some eighty-five thousand. This was pretty much the headcount levels I had dealt with at Ford before entering the service.

Because of the position I was in, I was able to reject reassignment requests that came my way late in my army career. While I had been initially responsible for initiating such transfer requests, their response came either too late to consider, or for that matter were set aside by my superior officers, General Philoon or his adjutant general Major Noel F. Thoralsen. In any event, I was able to maintain the status quo for personal purposes until such time as I had met the prerequisites for discharge under the army's point system. Unlike many, I was in the unique position to determine when the system called for personnel discharges and as such, I was not required to seek and await the different levels of approval. When my category in the point system came into play, I prepared and had my superiors sign off, and I was officially out. As a sidebar, let me mention that I was instrumental in effecting the reassignment of Major Thoralsen my superior, a grand older regular army officer, to one of the best army locations in the United States: Fort Lewis, Washington. He came through with his promise to me that if reassigned to Fort Lewis, he would send for me for assignment to the same facility. His correspondence to me confirmed the thinking, and above all were his comments that he was very pleased with the transfer, he was assigned the inspector general with a staff car and his duties were the best he had in a long regular army career. I hadn't heard from the major thereafter or since. He did make the offer for a transfer in my behalf, as he said he would. However, I was too close to the point accumulation system and discharge and couldn't accept, so I thanked him.

On a personal note, I am thankful for having been assigned to a single facility for as long as I had been, and grateful for the administrative capabilities which upheld my retention, and for those I had worked with during this period. My friends and associates from earlier times in the service, whom I had trained with in basic training, were dispatched overseas in short order, and, most unfortunately, many met their downfall in the first assaults in the Italian theater. I was not initially aware of this, but learned of it years later. There, but for the grace of God, in 1943 would have been my calling.

It didn't take long for me to get back into the swing of civilian life when returning for reinstatement to the employment office at Gate 2. As in prior episodes, programs were either being introduced or concluded within the office. The alien registration program, which I had left from, no longer existed as an entity unto itself. The program requirements for the most part were handled by the employment interviewers, with assisted standby personnel as the situation may have required. The tire rationing and share-the-ride programs were pretty well, with some exceptions, on their way out. That which was in high gear within the office was the need to get those employees who had bid on and gotten war contract jobs, slotted back into the regular complement of the workforce. Those without a basic job to return to were either offered available work or laid off. A steady stream of people were exiting the Ford Motor Company at the time, particularly women who had come aboard, did one particular type of work, and now that the work was over they had no seniority to exercise against others, and out they went. The whole arena was like shuffling a deck of cards slotting in those that had basic rights, bumping out others for the lack of seniority versus those returning from war work, and as necessary terminating those without retention rights. I left the company when people were coming in from all areas of the city, state, and country, and now the reverse was happening—some were staying within the area they now called home, others were returning to their out-of-state homes reluctantly, while others were returning to their friends and homes and looking forward to it.

Entwined in this mix were the returning service personnel, most of whom had re-entry and reinstatement rights. I had all the required documents for return reinstatement and chose to exercise this right rather immediately, rather than to await a long period of unemployment compensation. I found myself in the midst of a hodge-podge of mixed activity within my former office. While my objective was to get things leveled out and returned to whatever was considered normal, I was somewhat surprised to learn there were those who sat comfortably by, within the office during the war years, and appeared reluctant to identify the

return rights of the individuals from service. They had it nice and didn't want interference. In effect, most were fearful of their own employment displacement. I dismissed their superiority attitude and matched my winning wits and credentials with those looking for the challenge. Their position lacked substance and was from my perspective merely set aside.

**That's me at the hiring desk after
returning from the service.**

CHAPTER 15
HENRY FORD II IN, HARRY BENNETT OUT

When I returned, I was assigned to the interviewing desk, in the area where formerly the thugs and Mr. Harry Bennett's henchmen guarded the arena. Young Henry Ford II had already been released by the Navy from his assignment at the Ford Naval barracks, Gate 10 of the Rouge complex. After the 1943 death of young Henry's father, Edsel, the senior Henry Ford had taken up the reins of the company again. However, upon the urging of Mrs. Ford, young Henry's mother, her father-in-law gave up the responsibilities and turned the business over to Henry II to operate after the war. The transition was in effect with a new member of the family directing the business.

Young Henry had his own team now in command, with Mr. Bugas, formerly of the FBI, and formerly hired under the Bennett banner, directing the strategies. The entire employment office had been cleared of the characters working for Harry Bennett, including the open access to the drinking fountain, now that the keeper of the fountain was also out of the picture. Reviews had been in progress prior to my return to determine the alliance of specific individuals, and if connected with the former regime, remotely or otherwise, they were gone.

Unfortunately some got caught in this web without having been under the Bennett banner, and they got caught without the possibility of appeal. If you were identified in some fashion or other, you were gone. If, on the other hand, there was doubt as to your affiliation, you were cautioned and put on your best behavior. We came to understand that Tom Silvester may have fallen into the latter category. This was merely the assumption of those still there and I, for one, was very pleased he hadn't been caught in the net, and I told him so.

The retention of Johnny McIntyre, my former supervisor and alien registration overseer, I'm sure was based on his ability to convince, and properly so, he had nothing to do with the clique and as such he was salvaged. Johnny ended up at the Gate 4 complex as a supervisor on building maintenance. This was the area where the battle of the overpass was fought. Personally, I was pleased he was still working, and I felt the job assignment was much better for him than the clerical responsibility he suffered under. As for Mike, I don't know what happened to him. I think I had him on the road to recovery, maybe, and hopefully he's cleaned up his act and himself and also hopefully has changed and is doing well in some other vocation.

I'm getting a little ahead of myself again, and before going too far astray, there's a story that better depicts Harry Bennett, as if I hadn't already given you chapter and verse on him. I was asked to go to the main office, the basement area where Mr. Bennett's secluded office existed. I knew the area well. The purpose of my assignment was to hand deliver a document for Harry Bennett's signature and return it. Here we go again, I'm selected for the mission and don't know why. Someone thinks either I know him, or if anyone is to get the axe, it'll be me. Nonetheless, it was an assignment and I'd see to it that it was carried through. Upon arriving at the main office and heading for the Bennett area, I was met by one of his aides and escorted to what was in fact his indoor pistol target range. I was told to sit and wait and I would be called when Mr. Bennett was ready. The pistol range was directly across from his office area. Down the corridor were the offices of John Bugas, Bob Ross, and other distinguished gentlemen from the FBI who had been hired into the Ford Motor Company a short time before.

After waiting in this long chamber, I began wondering if I was destined to be the next target or if someone had forgotten me. Again, as in past experiences, I convinced myself things would work out and I'd accomplish my mission and be on my way. About this time there were many thoughts going through my mind, but the door suddenly opened and I was asked to follow a Bennett aide to his office. In that I had been instructed to give my envelope to none other than Harry Bennett, I made my objective clear to those that had asked, and as such, I was escorted to his inner chamber. Once there, I handed Harry Bennett the envelope, advising him that his signature was needed. In my absence of knowing what the document was, I couldn't point to where he had to sign. He looked up at me saying, "I know you."

I don't know where he thought he knew me from, unless he had a vivid memory and recalled my brazen introduction when he visited our office, or quite possibly through the grapevine network identifying me with the employment office. Wherever it was, I let it rest. He seemed to know what to do with the document as he removed it from the envelope. I stood at his desk and waited. He tried to sign once, then again, and again and again, but the pen didn't work. In those days we didn't yet have the felt or ballpoint pens. He was getting frustrated and it was obvious. The pens of the day were the ones with the little balloon ink retainers. He snapped the metal lever on the side of the pen, but no ink came out. At this point he hurled the pen — really hurled it — across the room, narrowly missing me, and yelled loudly at his clerk, "Don't you ever give me a pen again unless you've checked to see if it's full!" The pen stuck in the wall, and what little ink there was inside splattered against the wall. He proceeded with another pen to sign and retuned the document to me. I have no idea what he signed and couldn't care less.

While I'm relatively certain the document I had given Harry Bennett had nothing to do with his demise from the company, none the less and shortly thereafter, Mr. Bugas, with the FBI background and now at Ford, was called upon to handle the dethroning and exiting of Harry Bennett. This is a story unto itself, and I personally felt its handling by Mr. Bugas to have been tactful and quite courageous to say the least. He was surrounded by his hand-selected staff, also from the Detroit FBI office. He describes it best in another publication where he comments that, after telling Mr. Bennett he was all through with the company, he could have anticipated a knife being thrown at his back as he walked out of the office. I must add there is some uncertainty as to who actually informed Harry Bennett he was all through with the company. Some say it was young Henry himself who walked into his office and told him he was done, while the version we received was that it was Mr. Bugas. The book *Ford* by Booton Herndon speaks to it being Henry Ford II. Personally I prefer to think it was Mr. Bugas, under the direction of Henry Ford II and his mother, and not Henry Ford II himself, as I have mixed feelings of Henry's capability to have undertaken such a bold venture as this. The thinking that Mr. Bugas did the dirty work was shared by many within the company, particularly within our office.

CHAPTER 16
WAR PRODUCTION ENDS

T hings were happening fast now that the young Henry slate was officially in power. Remaining executives who anticipated being called in for interview and possible termination were leaving without waiting, as now their benefactor and sponsor Harry Bennett was out. Another program was being launched at this time, one that should have been initiated long before but never was fulfilled. For the first time, Ford Motor Company was calling in all of its major executives from all parts of the USA and all foreign locations. The purpose of this was to establish bona fide personnel records on each. The relationship these people had with the company bypassed all established rules for being on the payroll. No personnel records on them existed. They were major executives who had never been corralled into signing an employment agreement, passing a physical, having an established personnel jacket, or for that matter having a contract agreement with the company. Many of the executives being called in were particularly incensed for having to come to our office for fingerprinting, photographing, and signing a multitude of forms attesting to their employment with the company, including the issuance of star badges for those not having the badge identification signifying their executive status. Many of those sent for and appearing for processing arrived at our facility in chauffeur-driven limousines, arriving from all parts of the country, as well as from Ford facilities throughout the world. They were processed under the new rules of the company, signed whatever was necessary, and left for the most part in a huff. They, like the old timers on the Ford farms who were on the payroll, knew what was expected of them and did it. Their salaries kept coming to them routinely. Many of these people had been assigned by the original Mr. Ford himself. Their allegiance was with him and none other. Their existence was merely a line on a document from Mr. Henry Ford I, their pay came from his office, and their tenure, absent Mr. Ford's direction to the contrary, was assured.

Coincidentally with my return to the employment office after leaving the service, I was issued a star badge by Tom Silvester, for no reason other than the normal badge series for the office was not available. The star was not issued to me as a consequence of an executive role status, but merely as a convenient way for me to get into the building past the security guards and out. I've retained the badge, with fond memories, to this day. It was interesting to receive almost a salute from the guards once they spotted the star, as they knew what it meant. The lower the star number, the higher level of authority was its holder. Mine was somewhere in the lower middle. I have to assume that Harry Bennett, the Roushes, Sorrensons, as well as Dalinger and the like, all had very low series star badges. Regardless of the level of issuance, once you had a star you were in the category of prestige and much wealth. The badges, while discontinued as a series for issue, are collector items now. Every so often an ad will appear in the Ford newspaper, or in other local papers, offering a reward for a star badge. I have mine and intend to pass it along to the grandkids as a keepsake. I've included for this book a copy of the star badge, very highly regarded within the Ford society, issued to me.

Things had changed to a considerable extent when I returned. I wasn't quite sure who was in authority, what the scenario consisted of, or whether there was a program in place to handle the requirements. I was, in fact, surprised at the complacent attitude that was apparent and displayed by some with whom I had come in contact during my reinstatement processing. The fact that I had a legitimate military leave of absence, with a government mandate entitling me to reinstatement, seemed to be of little importance, particularly to those who had not gone to service and who sat in comfortable job positions only because they had not entered the service. The attitude seemed to be, "We'll make him a job offer, and that's all that's required." The obligation would have been fulfilled according to their thinking, and if I didn't accept, so be it. It was apparent what they were trying to do and I didn't go for it. I requested the opportunity to talk to my former office manager Tom Silvester, who I knew was still there. They acquiesced reluctantly, and about that time I'd had a belly full of

The enlarged picture portrays the Ford Motor Company's many-faceted activities, including the manufacturing element, the Rouge plant's eight famous smokestacks, the high water tower on the left, the airplane involvement, as well as the company's ships.

their holier-than-thou attitude and could have cared less. Frankly, they were either rejected from the service or had cut their own deals not to enter. There were many in this category comfortably secured in their own surroundings and caring less for people like me. Tom greeted me graciously and understanding I was ready to return, he personally escorted me to Mr. A.J. Miller's office, who at that time was still there and in charge of the employment office. Tom informed him of what my duties were before going into the service, what I had done while in the service, and of my current status. Before the day was done I was processed, assigned to a work area, and given a quick briefing of my new duties. It didn't take long to realize no job description existed and, as before, only through my personal efforts could I do the job and make myself an acceptable entity within the office. Again, this was Tom Silvester who bypassed all the red tape and politics within the office and got me back in the main stream for the future. As an add on, it was a good thing he handled my return as he had, in that I had returned long before my unemployment compensation entitlement had run out, and I preferred to be occupied rather than sitting around, as so many were doing. Secondly, I had been asked more than once to consider another army assignment, particularly officer administration training camp at Fort Belvore, Virginia, and the offer was still good. To avoid further temptation, I literally buried myself in whatever work was ahead of me, and in that way my civilian vocation moved ahead. I'll never know if the other direction would have been better in life. In any event, I chose the one I'm alluding to in this book, and for the most part it proved to be both interesting and profitable.

The war production was over and the factory was being converted back to its pre-war operations. Machinery was being dismantled and carted out of the plant. Thousands of employees were being identified for return to their former or comparable jobs, or laid off pending available work. Those without seniority rights — as I've said before, mostly women — were terminated. Late 1946 and 1947 were a trying and very mixed-up period. It was difficult to imagine whether things could ever go back to the way they were. It wasn't until 1948 that the first cars began to come off the "B" building line, later called the Dearborn Assembly Building. They were replacing the jeeps and amphibious vehicles that had been coming down the line throughout the war.

The government's huge aircraft building within the Rouge complex was in the process of being deactivated. This was the building where thousands of war workers were assigned in the production of the B-24 aircraft components, and where the engine test cells were located, testing the huge engines before transporting them to the Willow Run bomber plant for aircraft assembly. A majority of the employees in this facility of the company were transferees from other locations within the company, working as journeymen or upgraders, all making a considerable hourly income, with many hours of overtime, as well as the availability of afternoon and midnight shift premium. The money was big and so were the long hours. Employees were accustomed to the long hours they were required to put in. In fact, many worked the double shift—sixteen hours—from time to time. The aircraft building was one of several government wartime facilities within the Rouge complex, all geared for wartime production. Many of these were either turned over to the company or sold for a token dollar transaction to Ford.

It would be less than appropriate not to mention the experience I went through with one of these government buildings which had been turned over to Ford. The location was, as I best recall, the Mound Road plant, which had been vacated after the war and made available to industry. This was one more of the special assignments I had been assigned on behalf of Ford. My task was to hire appropriate startup office personnel for the location, establish an employment office for the plant, and commence staffing for plant manufacturing production. My liaison was with the Gate 2 employment office should there be questions. I was able to accomplish the startup objectives and as a part of this task I was required to find a suitable candidate who could take over after I returned to my home office at Gate 2. After much interviewing, I recall selecting a young man who had the maturity and knowledge to handle the requirements. His name escapes me now, but I do recall he stayed aboard and did an outstanding job for the location and company for many years thereafter.

What strikes me as somewhat humorous about the location was an aerial shot taken of the building from front side to back at a very low level. The pictures were developed and printed on the front page of the Ford publication and I also believe one or more of the local papers. The interesting thing was the pilot or photographer had accidentally taken a picture of the adjacent building and not the new Ford facility. Having been at the location for several months I was acquainted with the grounds and adjacent buildings and I knew the picture was not of our building. The picture raised no questions in the minds of those seeing it in the papers. I, on the other hand, chuckled at the error and called it to Tom Silvester's attention. We both agreed to leave well enough alone and let it pass. No questions on this obvious mistake ever surfaced, and we were just as glad it didn't. This little experience was just another true inside story, which has now been told.

A short time after settling back into the routine of things within the employment office, I was called upon for a new assignment to get acquainted with the employees of the Ford farms, specifically relating to their job content, assigned classifications, and identification series. The assignment entailed, in addition to going to the farms, reviewing with the individual employee what they were in fact doing, their understanding of the rate and classification status, and to respond to any questions or concerns they may have had. It was another most interesting assignment for me. For the most part the farms were located on the property bordering what is now the intersection of Ford and Evergreen Roads, and also extending from Greenfield to Paul on the north and extending to the Michigan-Greenfield area, where the Ford main office now stands. I often wondered what the huge tower was doing right in the middle of one of the pastures. The ultra-high tower, some twelve stories high with a red flag on top, was a project initiated, I understand, by Mrs. Ford. Her residence at Fairlane was not too far from the location. I had surmised the tower to be a police relay tower, or something to do with aircraft signals, but it wasn't either. I was told by one of the farm employees that if the flag could be seen at the Ford Fairlane residence, by Mrs. Ford, the proposed new central office building would not be erected at the location. She, understandably so, did not wish to be reminded of the trials and down periods she had suffered with the growth of the company. She wished only to enjoy her home surroundings, the rose garden, and her friends, without the unpleasantries of the fights, bloodshed, and past difficult times.

That area where the Ford central office building was to have been erected is today referred to as the Holy Mile, as a number of churches have since been built there. The main office, as a result of Mrs. Ford's wishes, was not erected on the corner of Evergreen and Ford in Dearborn, but rather at Michigan Avenue and Southfield, approximately one mile away.

Unlike the typical shop-oriented employee, the farm personnel treated their employment quite differently. The farms they felt belonged to them and they'd take care of whatever the needs were. These people not only resided on the grounds, in homes Mr. Ford had provided, but knew when the plowing was to take place, the planting time, and the harvesting. They were, to say the least, very dedicated to the needs of the Ford family and the care required of the farms. They harvested the food for the Ford table, including the chickens, eggs, and milk. The dairy barns were located just off of Evergreen Road, and a more interesting operation I had never seen. The cows had their individual stalls to return to each night and for milking. The barn was very clean—the cow manure never hit the tiled floor. Floor belt conveyors automatically removed the manure from the building and out to waiting bins for subsequent use as fertilizer on the farms. Each cow had its own drinking fountain. The weight of its head on the circular shutoff would activate the flow of water and the cow drank to its heart's content. Things couldn't have been better for a good night's rest for the cows before returning to the pasture the next morning. The farm employees handled the cow barn requirements quite routinely before going no to other needed chores. I found extreme loyalty to Mr. Ford and the farms to be the case with each individual I met.

The food they harvested was for the Ford family, and this was uppermost in their minds. Any surplus they shared. There was so much there that no cause for selfishness could possibly arise. In fact, they offered me freshly picked tomatoes and welcomed my early return. Through the half dozen or so visits to the farms, I learned more than I had ever hoped for. I got to know each employee as well as their supervisors, who in fact were as much farm workers as the rest. The contingent of farm employees was not included in the union-organized members of the Ford Motor Company as a result of the 1941 strike. They remained independent and continued to work as such for as many as ten years. While they individually had many years of company service, they had not established recognized union seniority and were fair game for elimination. My personal efforts many years after leaving Gate 2 aided them with job retention at a completely different location until most of the former employees had acquired a sufficient age level with which to retire. The details of this handling were somewhat complex in that, with much negotiating and the cooperation of only certain local union representatives, we structured an "Occupational Group Agreement" which excluded the farm employees from an automatic bump procedure and allowed them to remain in a safe haven without being repeatedly laid off and then again recalled for work. It worked out very well and to this day I am doubtful that the employees ever realized what I had accomplished on their behalf or how fortunate they really were. I was glad to have been in a position to have helped. This is but another story from within which until now had been left unsaid. If the occasion was ever to surface again I would, for the sake of these devoted and loyal people, handle the situation as I did before. Perhaps their family members reading this book will better understand the way it occurred. If you wish to have details, please contact me.

CHAPTER 17
JESSE OWENS AND OTHER ATHLETES

Jesse Owens of Olympic fame, who had joined the company along with the many other star athletes of the time, became a good friend during this period. We frequently had our lunch together in the back room after purchasing the routine soup, sandwich, and small pie from the lunch wagon. Jesse didn't say much of his accomplishments, or of his lack of recognition from Hitler of Germany for his achievements in the Olympics. I for one did not relate to track and field and the closest we got to his sport was when young men from either the plant or the office came to me because of my acquaintance with Jesse, asking for an autograph and on more than one occasion asking if they could run with Jesse during his lunch break period. There is a side story of the arrangements I was able to set up with Jesse and his alleged competitive runners, and we all enjoyed the trials. More often than not I was the middle man and Jesse did run a short distance to help satisfy their curiosity. They were very happy as both Jesse and I were.

Jesse's accomplishments were not necessarily looked upon as outstanding feats at the time. There were many things happening that overshadowed his greatness and like many other renowned personalities, his time in the spotlight didn't surface until many years after his greatest achievement. People were just beginning to get out of the Depression years, a war had been fought, Amelia Earhart was still missing, and the uncertainty of the times precluded the recognition he so rightfully deserved. Jesse had a job and income, and he went about his daily life like the rest of us.

Jesse was a good-looking, light-skinned black man who fit right in with the group. He was very neat and conservative in his attire and his shoes were always polished. He was easy to talk to and worked with people of the sociological office. By nature of the group's responsibility, he spent the greater portion of his time on lien resolutions or welfare cases. Of interest to the reader, and perhaps to the descendents of both Jesse and Jim Thorpe, is that both these renowned persons worked in the same office area, at the same time, in different capacities — Jim as a plant security officer and Jesse in the sociological activity. There is still another story to cover with the reader as it pertained to Jim Thorpe which I will put on hold until the appropriate passages within this book.

For an extended period, I was being put on special assignments within the office. Fortunately, each of these was quite diverse from the routine interviewing, hiring, and processing requirements. My normal and periodic station by this time was at the hiring desk. This was the job assignment I had as a personal objective and thanks to Tom Silvester, I finally got to where I wanted to be assigned. Yes, I did have the opportunity to interview many candidates for employment, and yes as a follow-through of the promise I had personally made to give some of the old timers an opportunity they otherwise would never have had, I was able to fulfill my personal promise. The truth of the matter is that there were hundreds of prospective employees being referred for consideration. Between Howard Holmes—a personal friend and fellow employment representative—and me, we handled the bulk of applicants coming through the line, starting at the beginning of each day until quitting time. While there were others ultimately assigned to the hiring desk, we did most of the processing. On certain days coming to work, we were able to determine the approximate time the personnel traffic flow would lessen, based on the lengthy lines waiting for job interviews. Sid McKenna, a close friend, subsequently joined with the hiring responsibilities within our office and ultimately progressed to much greater assignments both in and out of state, leading to his ultimate assignment as one of the company vice presidents.

Fortunately we were capably assisted by the prescreening that was being done prior to directing the applicant to our respective desks for employment determination. For example, the application for employment had been prescreened in the lineup for employment in the bullpen area. This prescreening, by the way, was done by others than the individual who was selling cars to the unsuspecting job applicants, earlier mentioned in this book. The crooked car salesman was no longer there, and obviously was caught up to and dismissed. The applicant for employment was, without his or her knowledge, coded, identifying race, color, and sometimes job interests. During the referral routing, the applicant's employment status with the company was being checked. If he or she had been previously employed, the record was pulled from the retention files and it would automatically arrive at my desk, or at one of the other interviewers' desks, simultaneously with the applicant. If the applicant chose to use a name other than their own, this too would surface, and without the knowledge of the applicant. This ploy was frequently used by the individual who had been discharged from the employ of the company and came to a screeching stop when confronted by the interviewer.

Jim Thorpe, one of the greatest athletes ever, as I said before, also worked with us. I'll tell you my story of Jim now. Jim, as a security guard, was frequently assigned to the employment office. His responsibility within our office was to direct the line flow to the respective interviewers, and perhaps more so, to maintain orderliness among those in the lineup entering our office as well as redirecting those not qualified for the available job openings to the exit areas. The attitude of some of the applicants after having been told no employment existed, based on experience, or to return at a later time, became violent, in fact threatening at times. Most accepted the rationale and understood the circumstances. Howard Holmes, who sat directly across from me, can easily attest to some of the confrontations both he and I were innocently subjected to resulting from applicant rejections. One of the major confrontations which I unfortunately experienced occurred right at the hiring desk, and much to my regret, was as follows.

An applicant under the heavy influence of liquor sat at my desk, insisting that he be given employment. He should have been screened out at the bullpen area or perhaps picked out by Jim Thorpe, rather than being permitted to remain in the building. After I detected his condition and attempted to persuade him to leave the area and try again at some future date, he unfortunately became adamant and insisted that he wouldn't leave until a job offer was made. I tried again to calm him down, even though it appeared useless and there didn't seem to be further use in trying. He was getting loud and completely out of control. He was a big guy and could have torn the office apart and me with it. My defense was nothing more than conversation and if worse came to pass, I had the telephone on my desk that I was already edging closer toward. If necessary, it would have served my purpose to knock him for a loop, or he in turn could have cold-cocked me. I was ready. Jim Thorpe from his entry door position watched carefully and was aware of the difficulty I was having with this man. Jim came over to my station quietly and while not asking me what the trouble was, proceeded to ask the applicant to leave, pointing to the hallway exiting path. He, the applicant, became loud, belligerent, and abusive in language, now against Jim. What happened next is for the storybooks. With one fell sweep, Jim grabbed him by the nape of his neck and lifted him up and out of the chair, and while Jim attempted to steer him toward the exiting aisle way, the man in his drunken stupor fought to get away and was literally thrown through a glass partition separating our area from the desk of our telephone receptionist. He slid across her desk and onto the floor on the other side. She was seated there. He got up and apparently in a sober moment brushed off his clothes — surprisingly he wasn't even cut — and walked out of the building. He was not forced to hit the glass, but rather, by his contortions in trying to break the hold Jim had on him, he had twisted himself in that direction, causing the scary scene. This person, whoever he was, made a big mistake in trying to match his strength with those of one of the greatest athletes ever. This is just another story that up to now has been left unsaid. I'm relatively certain there aren't many persons, including the families of Jim Thorpe and Jesse Owens, who were aware that here we had two champions of Olympic fame working in the same area and at the same time. The handling by Jim Thorpe of the drunk seated in my interviewing chair, was too much for me for that day, as it was for our receptionist, Marian; we both left for the remainder of the afternoon.

Now on with the story. We were having lunch at one of the few decent restaurants in the Dearborn area. I remember it well with its glass dome ceiling. The period was the winter of 1947. The eating place was filled to capacity with mostly Ford people rushing through their lunch. Most of the patrons just sat on stools around the serving counter, and most of the customers had their coats on, as you didn't have much time to find a coat hanger and get back to the counter, which was just as good, as it was a cold and blustery day. The restaurant was called Captain Johnson's and the owner seemed to know most of the patrons by their first names. Now we can cover the details of my visit to Captain Johnson's restaurant and specifically as I said earlier in the book, the episode with Mr. Miller, the former employment manager of the Ford Motor Company. The food was good and served quickly, and with thirty minutes or possibly forty-five if you were in the company of supervision, you ate and ran. Captain Johnson's still stands today, however it's no longer an eatery but rather a jewelry outlet. I was having lunch on this particular day, when someone tapped me on the shoulder, asking that I as well as the others extend to him a helping hand. The person was unshaven, in dirty clothing, and generally unkempt. I recognized him as Mr. A.J. Miller, the powerful executive of the Ford personnel office, the man we had worked for, and most recently the man who had again endorsed my return to the employment office after my return from the service. I was shocked to say the least. I didn't know what had happened to him in the relatively short time since I returned, nor had anyone commented as to where Mr. Miller had gone or of his status with the company. These questions in my mind were not uncommon, as the mix of executive personnel coming and going was at the time quite normal. I was obviously quite naïve as to what had happened to him, more so it appeared than those I was having lunch with. I was told to ignore this man and pay no attention to him. It seemed they were fearful of making a contact. They were unwilling to entertain further conversation with me on my concern, and it was apparent much was being left unsaid. Nonetheless, I reached into my pocket and pulled out the first bill, which was a five-dollar bill, and put it in Mr. Miller's hand. He didn't say a thing, and I for some reason felt he couldn't, but to this day I remember the tears in his bloodshot eyes when he looked up to me and nodded his head as if to say thank you. I didn't have much of a lunch that day. No one volunteered comment as to what had happened to Mr. Miller nor of what their relationship was to his apparent demise from the company. Now if this wasn't Mr. Miller, who was he?

Mr. Miller was a proven major executive of the company, with responsibility extending throughout Ford and the community. I had been of the opinion he was an honest person, good family, in fact as I recall his brother, a Catholic priest, visited with him in the office on occasion. To this day, beginning with the in-house and apparent controversy in the relationship with Mr. Blott, I should have known he was ready to be swept out and must conclude that's what had happened to Mr. Miller. I have no idea what in fact did take place with Mr. Miller and for reasons of their own, my associates made no overtures of the happenings, nor of the ultimate status of this man. I know nothing more today than I did at the time we were having lunch at Captain

Johnson's. Hopefully as a consequence of this writing someone will enlighten me. Whatever is the case, my opinion will still be the same—he helped me on more than one occasion and all I can say is I wish him well and most certainly, better than the condition I saw him in last.

As had been the case during the most recent past, things continued to change within the office. The elder Henry Ford died about this period, and I recall quite vividly how the hundreds of plant employees just milled around in mourning at the Gate 4 plant entrance. No one said a thing but it was so obvious the feeling of grief they were experiencing. These were employees who for the most part owed their livelihood to Mr. Ford. These were the black employees who had stayed in the plant protecting the property while havoc was being played out on the outside of the gates and fences during the 1941 strike. These were the same employees who got fed each time a barge or raft was floated down the river into the Ford slip and out of sight of the pickets surrounding the plant. There was no loud talking or laughing, not only at the gate entrance but anywhere two or more persons congregated. It was a very sorrowful day for many, whether employee or not. Mr. Ford had died as the day he was born, with no electricity or utilities within his home at Fairlane, resulting from the earlier rains and flooding of the Rouge River adjacent to his home. He was gone, and even though the baton had been passed on to young Henry, there was deep feeling and concern as to whether he could in fact carry on where his grandfather had left off.

We also had our work stations rearranged from an in-line passing-through facility to an individual desk and work station for each interviewer. My friend Howard had left his job by this time as a result of the pressure to get a college education, which he did. By the way, Howard had missed the confrontation between the drunk and Jim Thorpe's effective handling. My status was somewhat immobile as I was living at home and attending college in the evenings. Tom knew this and I believe he had much to do in offsetting any pressure that would have come to bear on me via our new manager. My desk under the rearrangement came to be located directly across the aisle way from his glass-enclosed fishbowl arrangement. I personally wasn't too appreciative of the arrangement because of the mentality of our new manager. I was of the strong opinion that this man was not people-oriented with the likes of a good personnel administrator. He boasted frequently of his mother's close relationship with Mrs. Eleanor Ford (Edsel Ford's widow) in the Grosse Pointe residential area, inferring for all to know, he wielded a very big club, and with the snap of a finger could get rid of or retain an individual. He could have easily misinterpreted the slightest innocent movement or gesture on my part as grounds for question. I ignored his presence and continued my interviewing assignment as though he weren't there. I apparently passed the test as he never questioned what I was doing nor had I been called into his office, like many, to explain my position on a given situation. Nonetheless, the indirect pressure was there and I, along with the many others in the office, did not enjoy the atmosphere and wished for a better work environment.

Keep in mind we were still in a period of job buying. It was not uncommon for a prospective employee to slip an envelope under the desk, as they had done to me more than once, with crisp twenty- or fifty-dollar bills. This was not my style, and in each instance I returned the money, whether in an envelope or not, and read the befuddled expression on the face of the giver, as if waiting to be asked to leave because of the attempted bribe. If the money had not been passed to me by the applicant himself, it was by his family member or friend who had escorted him to serve as his interpreter. It was difficult for me to return the envelope without being seen by my manager directly across the aisle way. The least indication of off-color activity would have led to question without understanding or explanation. Absent the possibility of detailed discussion on the money exchange, I quietly returned the money in the way it had been passed on to me and without embar-rassment to the giver. This was in line with my beliefs of helping those in need of help and an employment opportunity. I'm certain I could have resorted to this scam and made a lot of money carrying this lifestyle off. I didn't like this way of life and chose not to participate and returned the money being offered. Of interest were the comments which eventually came back to me: "If you're looking for a job, make sure you see that young blond kid at the third desk at the left." I was in fact fulfilling the promise I had made much earlier in life and extending a helping hand to those who I believed would be honest and capable workers and who hadn't gotten a job through sponsorship or payoffs. Added to this was the applicant who, because of his lodge affiliation, would tap his ring or lodge metal on my desk as a means with which to convince me he was a brother and entitled to preference for a job. The approach was rather humorous as I strongly suggested there was no way for him to be given preference unless he was qualified for the available job, and secondly his placement was dependent on job availability and his passing the interview. Once I got his attention back on track, we continued with the interview.

CHAPTER 18
MANAGEMENT
AGGRESSIVENESS SHOWING

To give you an understanding of the uncertainties of actions within the office, one of my associates was highly embarrassed as a consequence of a totally innocent experience that had confronted him. In the course of his responsibilities within the skilled trades area of assignment, he would have occasion to be discussing job content, location, etc., with an individual on more than one occasion, and as such would become acquainted on a conversational basis with the individual.

In one instance, the conversation revolved around deer hunting, with the applicant professing his hunting skills and expert marksmanship. The response, kiddingly, was, "If I know you, you couldn't hit the side of a barn with your shooting." This was taken as a friendly challenge with the follow-up comment, "I'll show you and bring you a hindquarter of the deer I catch." As it turned out he did bag his deer within the first few days of the season, and did return to the employment office carting this huge section of venison and, laughing, literally swung it around onto the desk of my friend. While all being done in good humor, little did my friend realize there was a challenge being accepted, and above all little did he expect it would be carried through as it had. This situation created quite a laughing episode within the office and much to the total embarrassment of my associate. From a distance, the commotion aroused the curiosity of our department manager who had limitedly witnessed the goings on, concluding by his unimaginative mentality that this carrying was a bribe. The situation resulted in Bob being called for total explanations of that which had taken place with apologies and embarrassment for the innocent act and behavior. Such actions unfortunately could have easily been misinterpreted as cause for dismissal. Fortunately discipline was not imposed, and that perhaps was as a result of Bob taking it upon himself to walk into the manager's office and tell him of the circumstances before being summoned for explanation. I don't know whatever happened to the hindquarter, nor did Bob my friend.

The point of this story is twofold: First, with the exercise of a little understanding, my friend wouldn't have had to go through hell in being called in the presence of the whole office for an explanation. Secondly, while the Bennett way of life had been supposedly eliminated, the prevailing attitude for superiority still existed.

My personal feelings had always been, since previously meeting the newly appointed office manager and assisting him while he was a minor clerk in the records section working in the basement of the main office, that he could have been a very decent person, had he given himself half a chance. Unfortunately, his demeanor led him in a different direction and I believe he suffered over this. Whatever it was I was doing or not doing proved successful for my personal purposes, as I was never questioned or called to explain the positions I had taken. The proof of my silent and good relationship came to bear when he asked that I visit the factory plant manager's officers as often as possible to determine what they needed in the form of personnel requirements, and to familiarize myself with their needs. While other personnel representatives and I did in fact previously routinely follow this ritual, I was pleased for my purposes, that he had endorsed the concept. He was coming around.

Following this lead, I worked out a plant visit schedule with Tom Silvester, who coordinated my arrival day and time with the particular plant manager or his operations clerk. I, along with others from the employment office, as time permitted, would visit with the plant manager and/or certain staff members of his, and discuss the problems they were having with their personnel requirements and what we could contribute to resolve the problem. This not only cultivated a strong personal acquaintance with the lead man himself, but paved the way to go directly to the job operations and see how the job was being performed and under what conditions. There were many job operations I became personally acquainted with and could easily relate to when the requisitions came to me for filling. I could make a rather quick comparison as to the job needs versus the applicant being interviewed for placement.

One of the highlights of this at-sight job knowledge came into being when an associate and I reviewed one of the operations in the plant motor building, located on Miller Road proper, one of the massive facilities within the huge Rouge complex. This facility had hundreds of people working on motor assembly and related operations. This was a tough environment to be working in. The men in most of the departments worked side by side, with no air conditioning or fans. The windows high above the work areas were rusted shut and hadn't operated for years. In effect, this was a shameful manner in which people were literally forced to work. It was either suffer the consequences or not have work at all. The employees relied on water and salt pills to tolerate the working conditions. The heat and production pace were totally exhausting. The men were passing out or being carried out on stretchers because of the unbearable conditions. While the work was of a light parts-assembly nature, it was difficult for many. The department number was 532 and considered one of the better job assignments. This may have been true in the winter months, but in the summer heat, with no ventilation, it was unbearable. And we were merely walking through, not working.

I'll take a moment's pause, now that we're on the subject of the motor building and the unbearable working conditions existing in the summer months. I happened to be invited by the plant manager to accompany him on a short tour of his facility, geared toward better understanding his operations and personnel needs. It was hot and smelly—the medical department had its hands full assisting employees who were passing out on the job or carrying those who couldn't take the unbearable conditions out of the building. In our tour we happened across a floor supervisor having an argument with the union's building president. The crux of the heated exchange centered on getting some fans or opening up the windows. The union president approached us, pointing out the problem the employees were having with the totally unbearable working conditions, claiming he couldn't stop a total walkout. Remember I told you earlier the windows high above the work areas were frozen shut from rust over many years of improper maintenance. The union guy saw us with white shirts and automatically assumed we had the authority to do something about the unbearable conditions. Mr. Patterson the plant manager listened while Archie Acaccia, the union building president at that time, was shouting and cursing at the top of his lungs. Charlie Patterson calmly walked to the supervisor's standup desk, picked up a wrench lying there, and the little guy pitched a perfect strike right through the glass window high above. He turned to the supervisor and merely said, to the amazement of the three of us, "Get the idea?" With that the argument was over and we walked away.

This little guy Charlie Patterson was dynamite. We next examined the crankshaft operations in our tours of this huge building, better known as department 498. This was where the greatest number of people were being hired and by the same token, a department with the highest termination rate. We seemed to be dealing with two extremes, the light motor assembly operations where the employees were having difficulty in the hot and humid work areas versus the heavy crankshaft operations, where the heavy machinery separated the work areas. Now here's the kicker, the cranks were arriving at the work stations by mechanized equipment, in this instance by hi-lo, with crankshafts loaded on wooden pallets. The load was placed next to the operator who cut the metal banding and let the heavy cranks roll to the floor. We witnessed the no-effort motion of the operator, classified as a lathe operator, and paid at a favorable hourly rate. What was unbelievable was that here was this little guy—about 130 to 150 pounds—handling an operation calling for the lifting of the crank from the floor onto the lathe and back down. The crank came in at ninety-seven pounds and was ground down to ninety-three pounds before being returned to the floor. We tried to lift the crank, both of us together, but it was impossible. Watching the operation we learned the little operator was not lifting, but merely handling the movement on the counterbalance. His foot would come down on the end portion and he would throw the crank with one hand as it made a slight counterbalance movement resulting from his bearing down with his foot. He repeated this to us several times as we watched, and it was apparent his expert handling of the crankshaft operation was due only to his long experience and tenure with the operation and not easy to come by. He enjoyed showing us how he handled his job and production requirements and wanted no change to lighter identified jobs. This man had been on the job for many years and acquired his skills only because he had to and survived while men twice his size and weight were unable to qualify. This was one of the job assignments that seemed to be automatically open because of the difficulty of finding men willing to stay on this type of work. As a side, a friend who was going to college had heard of this job and asked that he be given the opportunity to qualify. He was trying out for the college football team, saying muscle and endurance is what he needed. At his request and insistence, I assigned him to the crankshaft job where men half his size were working. I hadn't heard from him for about a week, assuming he was up to the challenge. I later found out, he had worked on the job only two days and was out trying to recuperate for the next three. He came into our office very meekly and asked that he be given consideration for a transfer, as he was unable to perform because of the heavy requirements. Understanding the dilemma and his embarrassment, I made the arrangements for job transfer.

As an end piece to my visit to this building I must recall for your benefit and mine the visit I had with the plant manager. He was a little guy as I've already mentioned, crusty in his attitude and capable, as he had to be in running the motor building, one of the larger operations in the Rouge, with its hundreds, if not thousands, of employees. My visit with the plant manager,

Mr. Patterson, permitted me to exchange thoughts on plant requirements. During our talks he excused himself as he had to discuss with a third person a production problem that had been called to his attention. He had already called the supervisors involved to his office, and was asking them to explain the problem. In the meantime the person raising the complaint, feeling he had the upper hand in the matter, proceeded to berate the supervisors without regard for the relationship between plant manager and his subordinate supervisors. They were highly embarrassed to say the least and stood in front of Mr. Patterson's desk at stiff attention. It was about then that the explosion occurred: Mr. Patterson wheeled around in his chair and in a loud voice, with finger pointed, shouted, "Don't ever again interrupt me and don't ever talk to my supervisors in that manner!" His talking to the complainant ended with, "I'll take care of my responsibilities and if there's any problem in the future you come to me." He turned to the supervisors, asked them to review the problem, thanked them for coming, and asked them to forget the incident. The walls were still vibrating from the scene that had just taken place. My mouth was wide open as I had just witnessed a most unforgettable situation and watched how diplomatically it was handled and concluded. He turned to me, apologized for the interruption, and asked, with a smile, that we continue our talking acting as though nothing had taken place. This little guy with the explosive and quickly controlled temper was the same man that eventually ended on the company charts as the president of the Ford Motor Company.

In still another instance at a different plant within the Rouge complex, I was asked to have another office person accompany me the next time I visited our glass operations. Mr. Lou Roth was the plant manager and was considered by most as one of the best glass men in the industry. He was always very willing to meet with me as it gave both him and his first-line staff people the opportunity to discuss their personnel needs. I had traveled with Mr. Roth through his very large operation of glass making, including a walk through the oven operations where the glass was boiling like molten metal and ready for pouring onto the long conveyors and glass-polishing operations. It was interesting to learn that the engineering of the long glass line had to take into consideration the contour of the Earth to eliminate the possibility of creating flaws in and on the glass. The company subsequently adopted a concept of glass flow invented in England. I introduced my associate to Mr. Roth and his group preceding a walkthrough with him. In that I had previously received the treatment, I asked that I be excused, allowing George, my associate, to go the distance. What this amounted to was a little game-playing on the part of the manager. He would walk you up the stairway and aisle ways leading to the furnaces and conveniently position you directly in front of the oven while he proceeded to tell you the temperatures, the chemical content, etc. He knew you were perspiring as you never had before and wished that he would end his dissertation and get away from the uncomfortable heat. He knew this and wasn't overly bothered by the heat while you, being unaccustomed, were dying a thousand deaths. My friend George, wherever he may be, will vividly recall the experience.

George also accompanied me, at the request of our management, to the giant boat docks of the company. Among the other, spur-of-the-moment, unrelated assignments I was being given, I was asked to oversee the personnel needs on the Ford ships. In that I had already acquainted myself with the captain, his officers, and crew, the trips to the dock and ships were not a new venture for me. The obvious purpose of George coming with me was to have a backup in the event I was not available.

Ford ships at dockside loading and unloading.

We arrived at the customary dockside position adjacent to the Benson Ford, one of the three ships flying the Ford flag, the others being the Henry II and the William Clay. The Ernest R. Breech, another huge ship of the Ford fleet, hadn't come into play until a later period. The loading ramp from ship to dockside was not in place. As such, I concluded the captain had ordered loading only via backside boat entry. In the meantime we were being directed by a man in a small motor-driven boat to walk toward a boathouse where he would pick us up. The boathouse, unbeknownst to us, was where Mr. Ford's personal cruiser was docked. We were asked to board the smaller craft and, after casual introductions, we assumed he would take us around to the backside loading platform. Instead and to our surprise, he proceeded toward the Ford area inlet. About this time we were bobbing in the middle of the Ford slip in rough waters wondering what in the hell was going on. Here we were all dressed in suit shirt and ties, and beginning to recognize a big mistake was in the making. We were laughing hysterically in the middle of this huge pond. The man who had picked us up finally told us he had been instructed to pick up two government men on the Ford docks who would accompany him on an inspection of the river area, the purpose of which was to determine the river pollution sources. We finally convinced him we were not the inspectors he was looking for, but merely two employees of Ford trying to board the Benson from its rear loading area. It was difficult trying to compose ourselves, as it was for the gentleman who picked us up for the short ride we had taken. He finally returned us to the dock, and we along with the boat person were all laughing beyond control as we glided back toward terra firma. His two inspection agents had not arrived for the boat trip when we returned and for all I know they too may have boarded the wrong ship. We finally got aboard the Benson and George was given the tour he had requested.

My responsibilities, by assignment, were to ensure that the captain or his first mate, when calling by phone, ship to shore, were provided the ship personnel requested. Once the ships arrived and docked, I provided either the captains or first mate with payroll data and other pending information. The assignment sounds relatively easy, but the truth of the matter was that it was trying and sometimes most difficult. Unlike the ordinary factory classifications relating to the job needs, I was dealing with an entirely different structure requiring certified and authenticated documents for each member of the crew and for sailing on the Great Lakes.

Making matters even more interesting and demanding were the timing elements associated with getting the properly qualified candidate for the open position. It was not uncommon to get a phone call at two or three in the morning from one of the captains on the Detroit River, as their ship approached the Ford entryway. Their message was they needed, by number, ordinary seamen, deck hands, etc., advising they'd be in at eight, begin unloading whatever they were bringing in, and out within a day or two. It got to a point that I found myself asking the captain what the hell he was doing by calling me at such odd hours and asking me to frequently do the impossible. Apparently they had gotten the word around that I would get annoyed by their odd-hour phone calls and they laughed about it and did it even more. They had a little game going on and I was used as the butt of their jesting. They knew that regardless of the difficulty in filling their requisitions, I would somehow deliver their requirements. My dad asked more than once if I couldn't get my friends to call at a more decent hour.

Fortunately, I had developed, on my own, a personal card file advising who would be on call and available. Again, unfortunately as before, I was given no training for the assignment, nor was there a script to follow. It was merely, "Go do it, I know you can." Apart from the already available merchant seamen with necessary papers, the calls made to me by young men who wanted to find ship employment were numerous. The fathers, in addition to the executives, who wished their sons could find a spot on the Ford ships, were many. Absent the required papers, I frequently had to provide the guidance and routing needed to obtain the documents. Once processed as a member of the crew, the pay was excellent and the working conditions the best, as was the food for the crew.

Those fortunate enough to become members stayed on for long periods of time; vacancies arose only as a result of illness or return to their own home ports. The fathers who had referred their sons, as well as those on board, knew they would be receiving good salaries and the best of food, and without sources on which to spend their pay. As a consequence, at the end of the shipping season, the young men terminated with a pocket full of money, and if they had handled their jobs well they most certainly got priority consideration for the following season. Because of the high incentive pay offered for those staying on into cold weather, many of the crew members who elected to stay on received bonus payment doubling and tripling normal income. Regularly assigned personnel officers and ordinary seamen were, at season's end, assigned to identified plant operations or assigned to ship engine teardown and maintenance.

The 1948 shipping season was a trial and error scenario for the Ford Motor Company and other companies owning their own ships. It was a question of their right to hire their own complement of ship personnel rather than going through the union hiring hall. In this instance, as I recall, there was a controversy between the two union organizations as to the representation structure of the ships' personnel. My job did not entail union involvement or positioning with their representation structure but rather, at the request of the ships' officers, getting them their personnel requirement before they left on their next assignment. The maritime regulations required all identified positions be filled with licensed or authenticated personnel—failure to abide by the regulations automatically committed the company to a monetary fine. I recall, because of the problem at times in getting people aboard, there were hurried calls to locate and/or qualify persons for sailing. The captains were quick to inform me of the mandates they were facing to ensure getting the full crew aboard. Sailing for more than two scheduled trips without the required number of ship personnel automatically subjected the Ford Motor Company to heavy fines, and the ship captains were held accountable. Well you know where that left me.

The Ford ships were the well-known and preferred ships by those awaiting shipping opportunities. They were identified as the best duty, clean, and well managed. As a consequence, it was not difficult most of the

Two of the Ford ships, always neat and clean, ready for unloading.

time to locate and place qualified personnel. I got to be somewhat of an expert in locating their haunts, or better still, knowing the bartenders who knew where I could rouse up the man with the papers I was looking for and needed. These exercises didn't allow for free time or a lackadaisical approach in getting who you wanted when you wanted them. Another part of the digest was where an individual knowing of the Ford schedule could bypass other calls for assignment and await his chances for Ford. However, they could bypass but once or twice before losing their eligibility for shipping endorsement and signing on with bona fide credentials. Their papers were like a passport of identification—without it you weren't going anywhere. My visits to the many bars got me to a point where the person awaiting call had fallen asleep or was drunk, and literally by pulling his papers from his pocket and making a quick determination of eligibility, I would whisk him off for processing and hurriedly get him to boatside for boarding. On more than one occasion, normal expedited processing could not be accomplished and as such, other means of handling were needed. The highlight of unusual processing occurred when, in addition to getting the person sobered up and readied for placement, the ship had already left our port. In telephone contact with the captain, I made arrangements to get the new crew member aboard by racing to the downtown Detroit docks, placing him aboard the Westcott II, the mail delivery service to all passing ships, and they in turn taking him to the middle of the Detroit River and from there on to the passing Ford ship. Once the sailor was aboard, the captain gave me his signal by a loud horn blast, acknowledging all was well. The captain was pleased with my service, I was personally pleased with the outcome of the venturesome task, and the new crew member, now that he had sobered up, was very grateful that someone had taken the time and effort to get him aboard the ship he had waited for. The Westcott II, I understand, had a wreck or sunk in the Detroit River in 2001. However, the mailboat company must have either salvaged the boat or built a new one, because the Westcott II serves the mail needs of Detroit River ships to this day.

For some reason the captain and galley personnel arrived at a conclusion that I personally liked blueberry pie. As a consequence of my delivery of the payroll data when the ships pulled in, I was always invited to the officers' dining area and served a freshly baked piece of blueberry pie. I never did object to the pie and coffee as we talked over the records I brought with me, nor did I explore the origin of the rumor. The pie was the greatest tasting one could ever have, and it was served, unlike what you would expect, but apparently by ship's custom, cut in one-quarter sections of a twelve-inch pie tin. You couldn't expect to get this treatment in any local eatery and I always let them know how much I appreciated their courtesy. Sometimes I wondered if this wasn't the captain and crew's way of saying thank you for my service. In any event, I like to think so. My thanks in turn had to necessarily go to the bar owners and bartenders that I met, for it was these people who saved me in locating the many qualified persons.

Before leaving this topic, I'd like to relate one of the more enjoyable experiences with the Ford ships. I was asked by one of the ship's officers if I wanted to accompany him aft past the many large loading openings to Mrs. Ford's private quarters. I knew she wasn't aboard ship, in that her little private elevator was not port side. Absent the walkway from shore to ship, the crew and other ship personnel used the Jacob's ladder for boarding—a long rope ladder with wooden steps from shore to the deck platform opening. When she did come aboard ship in her routine visits and after briefly visiting with the captain and his mates, her first stop was to the galley to greet the chef and attending personnel. One of my friends, and a good friend of Mrs. Ford, had worked in the galley and personally attended to her needs while she was aboard. Unfortunately he became embroiled in some union controversy and for his own well-being he had to leave the ship. She had made it a point to ask of his absence and, I understand, was told he had decided to leave the ship's service. This wasn't quite the true answer, as he subsequently worked with me and the employment office staff in finding suitable employment for others. Also worth mention was the fact that he provided me with many of the insights relating to ship activities, line of command, and protocol aboard ship. For all I know he may have been the source of information to the galley as it pertained to the blueberry pie.

I considered it a privilege to be invited to see her staterooms. One would hardly believe that here on an ore or limestone carrier, one of the most lavishly and beautifully furnished facilities existed for Mrs. Ford's private use. It was all designed in French provincial, in what by current nomenclature would be referred to as a washed tone finish, extremely ornate, however in very good taste. Only an accomplished interior decorator could, in my opinion, have the capability to describe the beauty of this setting. The Benson was referred by some as Mrs. Ford's private yacht. The reference was and perhaps still is appropriately considered.

Dr. Clark, a well-known staff physician and a good acquaintance within the employment office, as well as a long service employee, asked me what the procedure was to get aboard the Ford ships as a passenger. The

The Benson Ford

ships, for a short Great Lakes sailing tour, always had room for selected guests. I, in turn, passed the request on to the proper people and Dr. Clark was in fact invited to sail on the Henry Ford as the attending physician. The trip to the iron range was far less enjoyable than Doc had anticipated. Because of an outbreak of measles while en route, quarantine to quarters was ordered for those affected.

As the physician in charge Doc did what was expected of him and quarantined himself. He didn't get a chance to enjoy the scenery or the trip as he expected. He told me after the fact that he played a lot of cards with the quarantined sailors and did a lot of reading in his secluded quarters. On the other hand, the captain was thankful that the illness was contained and he had a physician on board.

Each situation and incident was another treasure in my learning experiences. Little did I know that my sole thought of getting a job in the Ford employment office would lead me to the experiences and contacts I was exposed to and learning from. The long and the short of it, and particularly for the benefit of the youngsters reading this material, I can say, stay with your objective. Things will change from time to time, and only your positive attitude toward whatever your assignments may be will serve to make enjoyment higher and greater objectives possible.

There are many more episodes which can be covered relating to my employment office experiences, but I believe we've already identified some of the more important features, while on the other hand there are still others that for the sake of privacy are better left unsaid. Before leaving my personal experiences during the employment office assignment, I am pleased to include the fact that I've had the opportunity to help many in their endeavor to seek employment at Ford and, unlike many others, I found it unnecessary to maintain book on those I helped, nor did I accept the many monetary gratuities that had been offered. Those involved in the underhanded practices were, as predicted, uncovered and released. I happened to come across one of these individuals as he worked at a northern Michigan campground. Regardless of his past practices and the fact that I had nothing to do with his practices, I nevertheless extended a friendly greeting, calling him by name. I was ignored completely as he chose to obviously remain anonymous. There were obviously an unfortunate set of circumstances he had created for himself, and he alone knew why. The attitude he chose to display negated and disposed of any further discourse from me on our past relationship. Whatever may have been his underhanded income from past practices apparently hadn't made him wealthy nor had the income lasted very long. By the way, he was the guy steering the unsuspecting job applicant into the "buy a car and I'll get you a job" scam. This too is for the benefit of the youngsters reading this material, and another lesson for those aspiring to get rich quick—it just doesn't work.

CHAPTER 19
PROMOTIONAL OPPORTUNITY DECLINED

It is difficult to go on to other items of personal interest highlighting my prior association with the employment activities, but as a finale I will mention that my relationship with the new office manager apparently was not as strained as I assumed it was. We never did have conversations on job status or problem areas; in fact, more often than not, there wasn't even a good morning as he swaggered down the corridor to his office. That was fine with me, and if he had problems, so be it.

He called me into his office one morning to introduce me to a gentleman I had known for some period of time. He seemed to be visibly upset when I informed him of our acquaintance. In fact, he was visibly taken aback when I told him that we had corresponded while in the service, but I didn't understand why he was upset. When he appeared to be better composed, to my surprise he made me an offer for assignment to the Ford Canton plant in Ohio as the employment director of this new company facility. The gentleman in the office whom I was acquainted with, Henry Aquinto, had been designated the Industrial Relations Director, and I would report directly to him. I was completely taken by surprise at the offer, as there had been no talk whatever of our office participating in this new facility, let alone anyone within the office being selected for the new position. I would have liked to find out how this decision had been made, what the options were if any, the duration of the assignment, etc. I got none of this, but again I kept my thoughts to myself. I thanked both my manager and Henry for the consideration and while not automatically accepting the promotion and proposed position, I advised both I would give the offer serious consideration and get back with my answer. The look of surprise was apparent on the face of my department manager, and what came across from this expression was the thought, in my opinion, that he was disturbed by my non-automatic acceptance of this major offer because in his mind, the general had spoken and therefore nothing other than a dictated acceptance would be in order. Nonsense.

I surmised that Tom Silvester, my supervisor, was behind it all, and after excusing myself from this non-arbitral setting, I headed directly for his office. I recall it was on a Thursday afternoon. Confirming Tom's knowledge of the offer, I informed him I was leaving for the balance of the day as I had some serious thinking to do. I left word with my parents of the happenings and that I was going to Canton, Ohio, to see what the facility and general area looked like. Once I got there I checked into a motel near the center of town and merely strolled around. It was late afternoon and apparently quitting time for the area's blue-collar workforce.

Quite frankly, the surroundings did not impress me, nor did the thought of being assigned to a heavy-duty manufacturing facility improve my thoughts. I already had two strikes against accepting the assignment, and upon return to my office, after my short stay in Canton, I had quickly made up my mind. In response to my commitment to get back with my decision by Monday morning, I informed the department manager that I had made my decision and once Henry, the appointed industrial relations director, had arrived I would be pleased to discuss my decision. I was summoned for my decision. I quickly informed both that at this time in life I was not interested in making the move offered, and further, while I appreciated the offer, it was not in my best interest. I felt obligated to tell them why, and proceeded to point out that I was attending school and terminating would not help my personal situation, secondly I was living at home and the expenses would have merely created a heavy strain on my financial status. Finally with understanding that a promotional increase would have been in the offering, I pointed out that the limitation of the promotional increase, under the company allowable criteria, would hardly offset the negative considerations of the offer. With that I thanked them and excused myself from the setting.

I well recall the blank and surprised expression as I left the office. I had made up my mind and wasn't about to be shuffled off to some remote corner of the Ford activity to satisfy a quick whim on the part of my department manager. My message was clear and because of his ranking, the ball was in his court. To my surprise, I was again summoned to the inner chamber, expecting the worst, but here again I was dealt another surprise. I was asked to make a recommendation as to who in my opinion could qualify for the assignment. I recommended an associate of Henry's, who I recall was working in one of the company's paddlewheel plants. My recommendation was quickly accepted and acted upon. A phone call from my manager to Marve went something like this: we've checked out the prospective candidates and believe you're most qualified for a promotion to our Canton facility, your director at the facility is, I understand, a former coworker, and together you'll make a good team. The answer was immediate, accepting the offer and looking forward to the new assignment. I was thanked and proceeded toward my desk. Tom my supervisor was in attendance throughout this trying ordeal. We walked out together and knowing Tom had made the initial recommendation for my promotion, I was sure he would have something to add in our talks. I wasn't too far from wrong as he quietly mumbled under his breath, "I'm hoping to be assigned to our California office in the very near future, and when I am, I'll not ask you, but I'll tell you you're going to come with me to California." My answer without hesitation was, "Don't ask, I'm going with you."

For the next several weeks my existence in the office directly across from the manager's office was pure hell. There wasn't even the benefit of a good morning or how are things going. The silent treatment was being laid on me but I was the one who knew and understood the meaning of the ridiculous scenario. I wasn't about to abort my convictions for a less-than-intelligent confrontation.

I knew the requirements of the office and my responsibilities. I continued to go about my business and did my job as it should be done. I was not impressed with the display of assumed knowledge and responsibility, nor was I impressed with the flaunting of my manager's repeated references to his mother's personal acquaintance with Mrs. Ford. This just didn't cut it as far as I was concerned. He had the authority to terminate my services or reduce me to one of the assignments of lesser responsibility. It was his call, and he obviously chose to defer any overt actions. The setting was not the best condition to be working under and I was open for change. Coincidentally, my manager was, by then, involved in a job change and I, in the meantime, was being strongly considered for assignment within the Ford Rouge complex working for a new organization being assembled as the nucleus of a nationwide parts and accessories operation.

The time was right, as was the proposed assignment, and when the final offer was made, I accepted, knowing full well the challenge was akin to the past uncertainties of what requirements would surface next. Before leaving the office, I was called by phone by the newly appointed manager for the employment office, Charles Columbus, with whom I was well acquainted. His comments were that he was looking forward to our new working relationship and he had hoped his appointment did not lead to my decision to leave the office. I was not aware of his pending promotion to our office and assured him I most certainly would have enjoyed working for him, and perhaps may have considered otherwise had I known he was to join the group.

My decision not to accept the promotional assignment that had been previously made to me for reassignment to Canton was, as I soon learned, one of the best decisions I had made since joining the company. From the beginning of operations at the new facility, there was nothing but problems. The relationship between company and union was strained to the fullest possible extent. The controversies covered the full gamut of possibilities: standards, safety, staffing, starting times, etc. Because of the major problems in attempting a smooth startup, the company plane was on a practically nonstop schedule of transporting labor relations staff personnel, engineering, production management people, as well as finance people, all of whom were being shuffled back and forth between Canton and the private company plane hangar at Metropolitan Airport back in Michigan. I fully realized it was not uncommon to start a new operation without gong through a problem stage but the Canton facility was far from a "jumpstart and go" operation.

Each day I read the local newspaper or the updates via company publications of the trouble at Canton, I thanked my lucky stars for the decision I had made

O.J. NORI

not to accept, and could only extend my well wishes to those embroiled in this mess for a speedy recovery back to normalcy.

The frosting on the cake occurred on one of my visits to our staff offices where I ran into my former department manager, the one who had made me the offer of reassignment. He approached me with extended hand saying I was absolutely right in my decision in not taking the proposed Canton assignment. He wished me well in my future with the company.

Sometimes the right decision is made and the uncertainty of one's decision is confirmed as right, even by those misdirecting or attempting to redirect your own way of thought. I never saw him again and understood he had been assigned a major responsibility in the Rouge production operations and subsequently retired to the east coast because of illness. I wish him well.

Now that I've covered a few of the many experiences that I was personally involved with in my initial exposure in the Ford employment office, I'll go on to the many other in-house experiences confronting me in the passage of subsequent years.

CHAPTER 20
THE MONTGOMERY WARD CONTINGENCY

Ford had hired a large cadre of executive personnel to literally take over and operate the highly profitable parts and service operations. Coincidentally with the company need to effect improvement in this large operation, Montgomery Ward saw fit to disengage itself from its tried and seasoned staff of operations people managing this end of their business. Sol P. Avery, then the president, saw fit to fire an entire block of what appeared to be qualified people. Included were vice presidents, managers, accounting people and all-around capable individuals. Ford, like the prior hiring of the whiz kids, picked up the whole lot. The chain reaction brought into play others from Wards, while not affected by the direct termination of their related top managers, were a part of the contingency also brought to Ford. It is important to comment at this point, these were people who knew nothing of the heavy demands of the automotive industry, the corporate policy, and operating methods. They were accustomed to responding to the spur-of-the-moment marketing trends, without their forward planning or inventory predictions. This marketing strategy was perhaps essential in their way of doing business, but the concept didn't rest well in predicting parts and heavy accessory sales in the auto industry. These were all the things I learned about their attitudes and way of doing business after I had agreed to accept a promotion from my former employment office position, to a confused and confrontational group of managerial people starting off in a multi-million dollar parts operation without insight into what they were involved in.

Adding to the confusion of this scenario was the fact that I joined this group with the understanding that I was to establish on their behalf a decentralized employment office activity and related functions. At least that was the understanding given to me. I was to establish an independent facility from that of the main employment office of the company. Supposedly, the concept was new, and ultimately each facility, whether it be service or manufacturing would operate as its own center. I was offered the assignment because of my background within the company and past proven experiences. It was a promotion for me with accompanying increase in salary. Well, it wasn't all that clearly designed. There was an apparent misdirected source of communications between my former employment office management and the new group of executives. They apparently hadn't though the concept through and didn't know how the concept system was to work. The commitment had been made and I was the swing man. It was too late to go back, and I was uncertain as to what was ahead.

Like many past uncertain assignments that started

on a negative note, it was necessary on my part to turn the situation around into something positive. I had no idea of what my new surroundings and management wanted or really needed. Again, the modus operandi was to listen and apply common sense, and hopefully the solution would surface. The person I was accountable to, also new in this arena, played the situation full circle. His primary responsibility was that of overseeing the labor relations between new management and the union. The union was a carryover from the main body of Local 600, the largest contingent of structured union activity within industry and the Ford Motor Company. They had all the answers, the seasoned table-pounders, and the clout necessary to call work stoppages, strikes, and all the grief associated by their presence. The identified labor representative saw fit to convince the new management that his efforts on their behalf were to be periodically at one of the many field locations throughout the country. What a snow job. They accepted what was being professed, and if examined, they would have known a ploy was in the making, allowing an enjoyable trek throughout the entire country on his part, without managerial reins to exist. Unfortunately while this gamesmanship played on I was left holding the bag.

Neither the union representatives, assigned locally, nor management understood or cared what the role of my superior was, as he traveled the countryside, or for that matter which I was assigned to handle quite independent of his role in the labor relations arena. The situation caused me to be identified as the representative to handle their conflicts, both with the union as well as their own supervisory and management conflicts. I became identified as their court of appeal in resolving problem areas. I was being launched into a completely different field of responsibilities and it became a situation, once again on my part, to learn and handle fast or sink. My nature caused me to stick it out, as I had done many times in the past assignments, and the answers would surface.

Fortunately, I had become acquainted with many of the managers in the various field offices of the Rouge plant as a result of my prior work area acquaintance, and my good relationship with them came to serve me in my hour of need. I called for their expertise in assisting me to resolve internal conflicts that were directed to my attention, and as friends they more often than not provided the guidance needed in the resolution of the problem. I was always grateful for all the help they had provided and shall never forget it. This not only got me over the hump in some of the most trying situations and without the help of my superior who was out gallivanting the countryside, but served as an introduction for me to the labor relations science. The hands-on experience coupled with the assistance of the professionals already in the field and the many hours of reading and college training carried me through one of the most difficult times of my career. Suffice it to say that management finally understood the holiday that was being enjoyed by my supervisor and he was reassigned to a heavy manufacturing job assignment back in the Rouge complex. He asked for it and got it. He was caused to leave what was considered by many a bed of roses, and eventually ended up with a midnight shift in a rough and less-than-desirable area.

Coupled with the difficulty I was having with my absent superior, I was forced to transact the daily controversies between line supervisors and the union representatives. Reference to the contract between union and management was not recognized by the assigned union representatives, as they were of the opinion they could operate independent of any written restrictions. It was difficult in my repeated attempts to identify and hold them in line. Much of my time was spent in re-educating them to the language of their basic agreement and in the meantime striving for an honest and working relationship to better serve the many hourly employees identified under the banner of this facility. At the time there were approximately three thousand hourly employees, and about seven hundred salaried workers, not counting supervision, management, security, and the like. The facility housed both Ford and Lincoln Mercury parts and accessories operations, later separated into two distinct facilities and operations.

While all the strife and bickering was going on between the union and our management, I had begun to cultivate a good and workable relationship with the hourly employees. They seemed to take to me and trusted my decision making. This, I believe, took place in one of my initial confrontations with the local representatives. Very much to their surprise, and with strong objections by plant management, I rendered a decision on a case in the employee's favor, as management was seeking strong disciplinary action against the employee.

The issue, as I best recall, was riddled with questions on my part, and no clear-cut answers were provided. I dismissed the issue and informed the supervisor and his manager, also present, that I wasn't about to be used for their strategies, and would rule against them in all such future cases. My intent was not to embarrass or call anyone down, but rather to stress the importance of an improved trust and working relationship between the parties. It wasn't long before the conclusions of the hearing filtered through the work force and I got feedback that it was about time someone got the supervisor and his boss, the general supervisor, to do some hard thinking before making unfounded accusations against employees. While I wasn't seeking such gratitude resulting from the position I had taken, I really was pleased with the resultant effects and said nothing more.

CHAPTER 21
DR. SHULMAN'S DECISION:
THE LADY IN THE RED SLACKS

It may be well to take a short break from the comments on the poor relationships that existed between the parties and address the reasons such difficult attitudes existed. To begin with, the location for the operation startup was designed to be the former aircraft building. This was the facility that during the war years was the working location for thousands of employees of the Ford Motor Company. There were individual test cells, where the engines were locked in place and tests were run and recorded on the various components. The area surrounding the cells were of three-quarter-inch-thick glass, allowing for visual observation while the tests were being made. I can speak to the thickness of the glass, as I was able to salvage a large section of the glass at the time the cells were being dismantled and had the maintenance people transport a section to my office for use on my desk top. It fit the desk dimensions just right and many times served as an interesting conversation piece, as its thickness was not a common covering for a desk.

The aircraft building was gigantic: a two-story building with creosote flooring and a superstructure to support the very heavy operational needs. In a word, the facility, the two-story structure, was not conducive to the needs of a receiving, warehousing, and shipping operation such as I was annexed to. The back end of this facility, as large as it was, served as the starting point for an independent operation, which ultimately became a company division unto itself, and it too was housed in a separate and very large building after the war. The building designated for the parts and services operations housed warehousing of literally thousands of parts and accessories of the company lines of vehicles. The front areas continued as administrative offices for the company lines of vehicles. The front areas continued as administrative offices for the company overall use, including classrooms for management and meeting rooms for the Ford executive personnel. The south side of the building housed all of the test cells for engine test purposes, while the entire length of the south of the building was laboratories equipped for ongoing experimentation and Company forward planning. By the way, the approximately quarter-mile long side of the building was the area Jesse Owens and I used for a race strip prior to my becoming associated with this operation. This was the area I previously spoke of where many of the youngsters wanted to race with Jesse and he accommodated them in their attempts to beat him. Unbeknown to most, there was a maze of tunnels and large connecting rooms at the lower level of the building, where the maintenance personnel conveniently seques-tered themselves for nap time, laundry washing, and whatever. As the overseer of building relations and related security, I had access to their little hiding place and didn't divulge or criticize its secrecy. They were aware of my knowledge of their little hideaway, and knew also that I would tolerate its being as long as it served no adverse relationship to the well-being of the operation and the personnel using the facility were ready on-call and as needed. The relationship allowed was much like my coffee-and-pie arrangement that had been set up at the Detroit Edison Company many years before. We got along just fine and again I befriended an entire maintenance department of some fifty to seventy men, and created no disruption to the objectives of the building or overall operations by keeping the entire operation under cover. I was particularly pleased by my relationship with these people and could call on them at anytime to get things done as needed and on schedule. You give a little and in return gain a lot.

My office was at the south side of the building, conveniently located within the center of the building, at the south side of the work effort, and adjacent to the facility manager's office and his staff. I had no complaints as I occupied what was once a plant security headquarters area. I had been given an outer office waiting area, a secluded inner area with an exit area, and unlike most, I had a private locker area and shower room that came with the territory. The story had it that this office, while being the security personnel basic mainstay, had been also known prior to that, as the central place where the plant manager had been physically escorted out by the union. There's a long story about the episode, and it served as the beginning of what ultimately became the selection of an umpire to settle disputes between company and union and also resulted in the first opinion rendered by an umpire, Dr. Shulman, as the prelude of setting the stage for both parties to abide by a decision-making process for the future. Now that I bring into play the name of Dr. Shulman, a thoroughly knowledgeable individual relating to people, problems, and attitudes within the work environment, I recall one of his first opinions registered in writing and as a part of the understanding and ultimate decision-making process reached by both company and union, it dealt with a case of a lady wearing red slacks. The case was remanded to parties for settlement in favor of the lady, with comments from within Dr. Shulman's opinion which, as I recall, spoke to the fact that there had been no specifications for articles of clothing, citing "common knowledge that wolves, unlike bulls, may be attracted to colors other than red and by other enticements." During this period of controversy, including the uncertainty of my own well being, the union officials through their friends and associates both from a union hierarchy standpoint, as well as their acquaintances within the decision-making body of the top labor relation arena, were gaining considerable clout, and frequently at my expense.

A copy of Dr. Shulman's Opinion A-1 is shown on the following page.

OPINION **A-117**

June 30, 1944

THE UMPIRE

FORD MOTOR CO. AND UAW-CIO

The Case of the Lady
In Red Slacks } Case No. 342 (Highland Park – 400)

A, a Highland Park employee, was reprimanded and docked one half hour because she wore slacks described as bright red in color. The objection was to the color, not to the slacks; the girls are required to wear slacks. And the objection is based on the safety and production hazards that would be created by the tendency of the bright color to distract the attention of employees, particularly that of the male sex.

Protection of employees against safety hazards by the publication and enforcement of safety rules is an accepted duty of Management which Management must discharge however distasteful the task may be to it or to the employees. If Management determined upon investigation that certain forms of attire tended to distract the attention of employees in a "co-ed" plant with resulting safety hazards and interference with production, and if it published rules prohibiting such forms of attire, it probably could not then be said that such rules were unreasonable or beyond the proper scope of Management's duties.

But such is not the case here. Neither the Company nor the Plant Management promulgated or published any rules as to the color of employees' clothing. The claimed general understanding that bright colors were "taboo" is no more definite than that. What color was proper and what color was

"taboo" was apparently a matter depending entirely on the spot reactions of individual Counsellors or Labor Relations officers to particular slacks as they appeared on the scene. And the claimed understanding was the product, not of the publication of a rule, but of alleged repetition by word of mouth and by diverse unspecified persons. Apparently bright green slacks were tolerated. And there was no effort at specification of other articles of clothing, or the fit thereof, which might be equally seductive of employees' attention. Yet it is common knowledge that wolves, unlike bulls, may be attracted by colors other than red and by various other enticements in the art and fit of female attire.

It is clear that there was here no effort to survey the field and to prescribe knowable and enforceable rules. The matter was left largely to idiosyncracy of circumstance and of persons in authority. That is not the way to prescribe or enforce rules of conduct.

A's reprimand is to be expunged from the record and she is to be reimbursed for the half hour lost in the Labor Relations office.

HARRY SHULMAN
Umpire

CHAPTER 22
ANNIE AT 13 AND OTHER
PROBLEM RESOLUTIONS

It seemed as though I was put out to pasture, without assistance, and expected to strike out, and my top experts would bring in one of their friends or seasoned experts to take over and resolve the situation. Fortunately, and by my nature, I never gave them the opportunity. That which hurt the most was when the union representatives, being well aware of the error of their position in a given situation, would tell me that they would get their way by merely making a phone call and I, in turn, would be told to back off. This was a sick way of doing business, and being the good soldier that I was, I followed orders, knowing eventually these types of scare tactics would have to end. It happened more times than I like to remember, and it took considerable effort on my part to convince the top level do-gooders to rethink what they were being subjected to, both in terms of the money and the games union representatives were playing. It seemed that for the longest time, while fighting in my attempts to bring a relationship with the union representatives, my bigger battle was to get top side to understand that their interference and politics served nothing but to cultivate a stronger resentment at the local level, with unchecked power given to a radical element. Unfortunately they seemed to be quick to render one-sided advice, but never to serve up constructive opinion for decisive and effective resolutions. The attitude that seemed to prevail was, "You may be right, but don't rock the boat." Nonsense. It was difficult for me to accept the cop-out in favor of the unwillingness to participate in a continued play with politics at the staff levels, but doubly difficult were the dictates to convince my own management of the assumed righteousness of the position that had been handed down. Again more nonsense. I cite these experiences only to show the young readers that my work and responsibilities were never a piece of cake, but often consisted of biting the bullet and necessarily moving ahead with warped directions. If you wanted to survive and fight another day, that's what you had to do, and while shameful in my way of life, I did it. Now after some four decades later I survived, I did in my later career years have the clout needed to put a stop to some of the double-talk being handed down, and hopefully my personal stand on many of the issues still stands today and may well serve to assist others. I point with pride to the arrangements I had introduced in getting the non-Ford outside contractors to get their requirements accomplished without interference by the local representatives. This handling became the way of effectively doing business and was adopted by most of the company locations.

As an aside, the work force within the operation was a sponsored group of personnel, either from strong union politics, which dictated the assignment, or in many past instances, the direct sponsorship of Mr. Henry Ford himself. We had people who, because of their past experiences with the law or their personal health, were placed in the operation. It was known as one of the best places for assignment, as it was a clean and healthy environment. The union was aware of this plum. They sought out and frequently succeeded in getting acquaintances assigned to the operation. One of Mr. Ford's direct assignments into the facility was that of a middle-aged lady who had contracted a disease causing her arm to grow in unusual form, twice its normal size. Her condition was referred to as elephantiasis. She had undergone numerous experimental surgical procedures, all paid at Mr. Ford's expense, and given a job as a records clerk where she worked comfortably and without embarrassment. There were many others including blind men who worked diligently all day at our packaging operations, with their leader dogs lying beneath the work tables, awaiting their owners' instructions.

During this period I happened across a record of one of our employees that left me somewhat confused. The seniority versus the date of birth didn't coincide. It was necessary to adjust all records to meet the company's new retirement policy. To eliminate possible error, I requested the employee in question to come to my office for discussion and gave no specifics as to the reason. She was a very good employee who did her assignments dutifully and with an attitude that was exemplary. I proceeded to inform her that I had occasion to review our records and couldn't quite understand her particular status. According to my review, her seniority date of hire with the company, in relationship to her age at time of hire, would have meant she would have been thirteen years of age, and that couldn't be. She was a middle-aged lady at the time we spoke, looked exceptionally well-groomed in her attire, and carried herself erect and with poise. She did not respond to my concerns. After a long pause she raised her head and commented that she had carried the secret within herself long enough and was pleased that I was the one who had uncovered the truth. I still didn't understand, and she proceeded to unravel her sordid story. She spoke of the time she had accompanied her mother to the Ford Rouge employment office many years before. Her mother was in need of employment and she merely stood by and listened. It was customary at the time for the women to wear fur-trimmed shoulder scarves, as her mother wore, and because of the extreme heat she passed it down to her daughter to hold. She said she had draped the scarf around her neck and apparently looked very much older than she actually was. She was well-endowed and even at that age carried herself well. The man looking down from the hiring desk, after having interviewed her mother and passing her for employment, asked if she was also interested in employment. She merely nodded yes, was given a handful of forms, and continued to follow her mother. She was thirteen years of age at the time and hired as was her mother. Her description to me of the hiring desk arrangement and the extreme heat within the area was familiar to me, having personally lived through the experience. If the guy was occupying his perch at the drinking fountain at the time, I don't know. If he did, he didn't know what was going on, as she as a job applicant merely went to her next processing station and passed that as well. At the conclusion of my reviews with her, I assured her I would not divulge her secret to floor supervision as she had asked, and her record would show her years of employment to be correct. She was very appreciative and after shedding a few tears she was totally relieved. She was also informed that no disciplinary action would result, as the company some years before had set the records straight. My promise to her was not divulged to anyone until this writing, and this has been many, many years since the occasion arose. Good luck to you Ann, wherever you may be.

Now that we are into discussion of one's personnel records, the status of Phil Somera must be cited. Phil was a part of the group from the Highland Park facilities that was amalgamated with the new Depot operations at their new location. In fact, Phil was the chairman of the union at the former location, and those transferring at the time he did (and there were many) continued to look to him to answer their concerns. Unlike the union representation he became affiliated with, Phil seemed to be a personable, caring individual, and as such, fell into the disfavor of the rabid table-pounding element vying for position at the new location. He, because of the strong support from his peers, was viewed as a possible threat to the ambitions of those who were attempting to comfortably occupy their new positions. As a consequence of our becoming acquainted, he confided in me and talked about a seniority challenge request he had submitted to the union, seeking seniority credit for past service. After filing many appeals, which apparently fell on deaf ears, his request was not acted upon, and no response was forthcoming. Under the seniority arrangement, the union was required to initiate the initial request for changes or adjustments. This was not to happen in this case because of the politics, and Phil was left out to dry.

Phil spoke of a conflict in his personnel record that he had lived with for years, and he wanted to bring out the circumstances and hopefully correct his personal status. It seems that many years earlier in his career with this company, he was able to continue his employment and income after being laid off and later rehiring under another name. Falsification of the records was known to be automatic termination without appeal or re-employment with the company. Many lived their entire working careers with hidden secrets such as Phil's, never divulging the circumstances for fear of losing job and income. By today's standards, it is difficult to comprehend how scarce a job was, and how protective one had to be in order to continue with a decent survival. People would buy a job from another for a price, and work on the job, in the midst of hundreds, without detection, and under the name of another, as though they had been there for years. As I said before, as in Ann's case, all records were being purged, as a consequence of the newly introduced retirement plan, and a moratorium was in place that was not intended to discipline or dismiss the employee, but rather to correct the misinformation existing in the personnel record.

I spent much time with this employee, his initial hire-in name was Fillipiano Somera and he was now Phil Somera. His claim was that he was the same person and initially hired in under his native Filipino name, and if someone would check his record he stood to gain some six to ten years for ultimate retirement and income purposes. His plight seemed to have been going nowhere. Based on the records, there seemed to be no substance to his request.

His story was logical, however there was no recorded support evidence giving credence to his tale. The records were of separate individuals. Any attempts on my part to automatically bridge the separate records would have been an outright violation of ethics and of my principals. I could not acquiesce and so informed him. From a personal point of view, I was not content with the conclusion and unbeknown to Phil I dug a little deeper. My research with the conclusion into the medical records of the company for the man known as Fillipiano. Recorded as medical evidence was a statement from a company doctor citing a deformation of arms at the elbow level. Not understanding what this meant, I called Phil into my office and, without divulging detail, asked him of any known medical background he may have been acquainted with. His answer was negative. I then asked him to roll up his shirt sleeves as I wanted to see his arms, still not telling him what I was looking for. In response to my next question as to any difficulty with is elbows, he clenched his fists and with associated muscular action literally flipped his elbows from their underside position to the top. I was totally surprised with this episode and not saying anything further told him to pull down his sleeves and wait. I called his union representatives informing them I was aware of the seniority challenge Phil Somera had initiated, and I was aware that to date no affirmative action had occurred. I asked them to witness as I had, based on the medical records of Phil Somera and the initially hired Fillipiano Somera, a unique occurrence, not duplicated by anyone I was acquainted with, nor was I sure had they. I asked Phil to come in and repeat the exercise shown to me, pointing out to the union that it was duly recorded on the medical hiring-in records, proving quite conclusively the two Someras were one and the same. There was no further question by the union, as the seniority in question was rightfully bestowed on the employee and the records in question were amalgamated for company archives as one.

Apart from the above and to give you some ideas of the various trying situations I, as well as management, had been confronted with, was the next classic. I had been requested to assist in the sponsorship of a financial collection for the wife of a highly thought of employee who had suddenly died. As a means of mending fences between salaried and hourly personnel, I requested a one-time collection of funds, involving both factions, and turned the money over to a group having responsibility. All went well, with a considerable amount of money having been collected.

The joint salary and hourly committee determined that the union chairman was the most appropriate individual to express the condolences of the work force to the wife and family of their former work associate, and to make the gift of several thousand dollars for their personal use. This outpouring of good intentions by both hourly and salaried employees was unfortunately ultimately misdirected. Several weeks after the supposed delivery, several of the associates of the employee decided to pay their respects, and to determine if further assistance was needed. They were thanked for the money collected and presented by the union chairman. That which surfaced in their conversation was the amount of money she spoke of, which was considerably less than that which was collected and was to have been delivered.

One of the old timers as a designated group representative, came to my office and informed me of their finding. It was a question of what they should do. Here it was their representative, the president of their internal organization, alleged to be involved in direct theft, and with the money from both the hourly and salaried work force of the location. My advice to him and the group was to take the matter up with the union's higher management, and in the meantime I would apprise them of the allegation for their expected actions. Without greater detail, I was contacted and informed that the union chairman was removed from office, and that was the last I heard from either the national Ford department, or for that matter from the culprit in question. He never did show up for work in our building, and it was a good thing he hadn't as there were both salaried and hourly employees who would have liked to work him over if he reappeared. The question of the missing money and its repayment was a matter for the national department of the union to resolve and I was not further knowledge-able or involved. There was however some feedback that the missing funds were in fact somehow donated by the upper levels of the union's internal funds and the widow and family were made whole. There was considerable satisfaction in knowing that the hierarchy of the union did in fact step up to their responsibilities on behalf of their membership, and took very definite action. This was a first for them in both instances: getting rid of the assigned union chairman and secondly going into their own cash reserves to correct an unfortunate people error.

The stories go on and on. There was my baptism into a most unsavory and unenviable set of circumstances, as it related to mending a relationship between man-agement of the facility and the assigned local union representatives, which appeared be hopeless. There was no assistance in correcting improved relationships, and I wasn't getting any assistance whatever from the person I was supposedly responsible to. In fact, his infrequent visits caused greater disruption to the relationships than ever. We were better off when he didn't appear, and we were much better off without his negative involvement. One would assume that the error of his ways would eventually catch up to him. Better still, his game-playing with his superiors was being tolerated only because those to whom he was responsible knew no better. He convinced his superiors that his way was the right way of doing business in the Ford Motor Company, and in the absence of being challenged, he effectively continued his ruse. I, as well as others, felt strongly that someone would eventually wake up and lower the boom on this self-serving individual, and it eventually happened. I'll tell you about it in later passages in this book. Unfortunately my central office staff did not intercede and the band played on. Interesting were the factual comments from their view point that they had expected someone at the local level would have taken appropriate corrective action once he had been reassigned from the responsibility to local jurisdiction. Again, we're dealing with a cop-out, and unfortunately from my staff hierarchy. In the meantime, the other side of this trying mess was the repeated attempts by the new management to get their way, regardless of contractual prohibitions or corporate policy. Here was a group of new managers playing games with the union, and my supposed leader encouraging them under the guise that it was the way things had to happen at Ford. It was a crazy setup and no one with authority was putting a stop to these shenanigans. Unfortunately, here I was out on a limb again without the needed backing. This was not the way I had learned to do things in the company, and I had to avoid the outright conflict with the guy I was responsible to while watching the Montgomery Ward people do their self-sponsored and frequently ridiculous things.

In retrospect for a moment, all of these things were happening during this period of transition: the change in management, the separation of operations from the Rouge, the consolidations of operations in the two separate facilities and going on, the uncertainty of the supervisory capabilities, confused and naïve management, the realigned workforce, thefts at the highest level ever experienced, an overly anxious representation structure without stops in their grievance writings, a security system handling their assumed responsibility unchecked and on and on.

I had an option. I could quit and try for other employment, a consideration I knew was hard to come by, or I could continue to try with the situation as it developed, and hope through the grace of God that things would get better. Well they didn't, and I was the patsy, trying to hold my head above water, without help, and taking a rough beating in my path of assumed righteousness.

It was not at all uncommon to find full containers of high-priced engine parts missing, or for that matter, find pallets of incoming cartons with the center portion gutted out, leaving only the four sides visible, referred to as "rat-packed." The temptation for thievery was great. The missing items amounted to thousands of dollars. One could reach into a bin amongst the thousands of small shining parts and put them in his shirt without anyone being the wiser. The unique high-dollar items placed in special bin locations were frequently pilfered and missing even before the stock status and inventory of the part and bin location was completed. I eventually found that I had to take the role of judge and jury on those apprehended or suspected of theft. The security force was having a field day in identifying or trying to identify thefts.

The security supervision even went so far as to place one of their own people on top of a bin in a four-by-four cardboard carton to observe what was going on below. In this instance the purpose of this surveillance was not for thefts, but rather to determine who the culprit was that was taking steering column rods, about three feet long, out of their storage bins, rolling them into the floor conveyor, causing them to ride beneath the floor surface until they jammed at the bend. This was very dangerous, causing work stoppages, considerable equipment damage including concrete eruption because of the pulling force of the mechanism as well as killing potential to the men next to the moving equipment. After several episodes of this crazy enjoyment by one or more of the employees, I, with the acceptance of the building management, dismissed all of the employees for the day. It happened again in the middle of the day and the employees were told to go home. Employees were disgruntled as they left the building, considering the loss of income. It got to the point that a select cadre of concerned employees came to my office and informed me that it would not be necessary for me, the labor relations effort, or security personnel to become further involved in attempting to find out who was involved, as they would find out, through their sources, and the guilty person or persons would have to be carried out of the building. There was no further sabotaging after the meeting with the self-appointed deputies. Those responsible for the countless hours of lost time to the employees and the operation were never identified. By the way, the lookout in the cardboard carton on top of the bin had to be carried down as he couldn't take the long hours of confinement, and it was believed claustrophobia may have gotten to him, or he may have suffered a slight heart attack. The ploy set up by the security management fell apart, as the assigned guard was brought down to the floor level by several of his associates, and necessarily done in the presence of the onlooking hourly work force.

It is difficult to recount the many labor cases that filed through my offices, or the number of grievances, in the hundreds, that were being submitted, which I had to resolve. It was a period of trying attitudes by management and equally an attitude of unacceptability on most practices introduced by management. The union concluded the operating conditions as they affected the hourly workforce to be hopeless. I was not at all convinced the Montgomery Ward disciplinary measures and general attitudes were the right or proper way of doing business, or for that matter their methods of treating people. They were archaic in their approach to people and in my opinion antiquated in their methods. There was a total distrust on both sides, and this was rapidly becoming an internally acceptable way of doing business. Without backing, I was having a most difficult time during this period in professing cooperation and honestly in the relationships.

To give you some idea of how strange the Montgomery Ward personnel's former concepts were in relation to the established way we did business, there was an instance when I was being ordered, and I mean ordered, to contact all local high school principals for a listing of available students who would be willing to come in to do some material handling or related work. The direction I got was that I should carry a listing of available students for immediate call-in as had been the way they handled their requirements at Wards. Logic had fallen on deaf ears as I tried to enlighten them about long lists of laid-off employees of the company who were entitled to placement before resorting to their way of doing business. I informed one of their executive personnel that I carried no listing of school principals, schools, or students, and I wasn't about to start. We parted company in short order, and his attempts to get me replaced were for naught.

The third side of this dilemma was power politics. The union was continuing to play, both within their own ranks and out, to gain a strong negative foothold in our relationship, and at the expense of doing business in the newly created separate and autonomous proposed large profit center of the company. Union muscle, table-pounding, and stubbornness seemed to be a way of life with many of the union's representatives, and it was most difficult to lend their thinking to logic and reason. The Packard Motor Company was a good example of the stressful relationship that existed between management and the union culminating in downfall of the company. I was at the receiving end for the requests for hiring consideration of a number of terminated ringleaders, names that I was familiar with, and declined to provide a haven for their further destruction. My relationship with those making the recommendations suffered greatly, but for everyone's well-being I did what I thought best. I was glad I rejected the sub-rosa requests. The other company that was going through tough times, with what seemed to be wildcat strikes every few weeks, was the Desoto plant of the Chrysler Corporation. Interesting in this regard was the fact that I became well acquainted with Jim Quinn, and in fact worked for him as he escalated in the ranks of Ford. He was the son of the union chairman that kept Desoto management on their toes. While I was not acquainted with his father, I can say Jim was a classic, and a finer person was hard to come by.

CHAPTER 23
THEFT: A WIRE BAND AROUND HIS WAIST

Getting back to the initial stages of my introduction with the new management of the Ford parts and accessories, and that of the aspiring union representatives, there are many stories to relate during this period. From a personal recollection, one of my experiences related to an episode that occurred just outside of my office, and shortly before we left the former building in the Rouge. I, along with other general office personnel who occupied somewhat makeshift quarters, was separated from the warehousing activities by floor-to-ceiling cribbing that ran the entire length of the building. The commotion on this particular afternoon aroused many of the salaried people working in their office area, who rushed to the cribbing to see what was happening. Well it seemed one of our illustrious supervisory chargers was convinced one of his assigned hourly employees was caught attempting wholesale theft. Joe, the general foreman, had wrestled the employee to the ground in his attempt to retrieve as exhibit "A" the material from the employee. There was a lot of kicking and name calling, and apparently as the employee got to his feet a band of wire nearly wrapped around his waist with a combination of spark plugs, motor points, and other small but unto themselves expensive and highly pilferable items fell to the floor. Joe was attempting to get them back around the employee's waist as he called for witnessing help.

Well, the next step was in my office with the union aligned on one side and Joe and his aides on the other. For my purposes the hearing didn't last long. There were no witnesses, and after hearing the general foreman's version of what had happened which, by the way, was reported as a premeditated plan by the employee for the removal of parts from the premises. I then asked the employee for his version and he merely denied involvement. His story revolved around the fact that he had seen a wire on the floor and as he was doing his job, that of a stock picker filling a bona fide dealer order, the general foreman happened by and accused him of setting up the parts for theft. His added comments were, "I don't know what he was up to initially, but when he wrestled me to the ground, I was merely trying to defend myself."

I asked the union representatives to leave the office as I did the general foreman and his people. While the union chairman didn't like the idea, I asked the employee to stay. I spoke with him on a personal basis, informing him that I knew he was guilty of attempted theft, and that I was certain he would again attempt the same act, and in that there were no witnesses to this attempt and his supervision had acted prematurely, I would let the matter rest. However, should it recur, I would hope that he understood he would be discharged and an umpire would make a further determination on this action and subsequent similar occurrences. We parted with understanding that his best position would be to self-terminate before I was forced to do what he knew was necessary. The general foreman was cautioned as to his premature actions. We had literally thousands of nice shiny parts in the warehouse and any man assigned as a stock picker could easily say he was performing his assigned work. The general foreman was told that a charge of theft in our warehouse could only be supported with fact. Intelligent caution and observation, without blowing the whistle, was a prelude to making a charge of theft stick. The man should have been watched as he left the building for one thing, and then apprehended, or secondly the matter should have been reported to our security personnel within the building, who are schooled in such matters and would have handled the situation professionally. While the general foreman didn't like the message he was getting, he did accept the rationale. His total satisfaction came in knowing the man had been again called down for attempted theft and based on our personal understanding left the premises without creating a problem. I explained that he was aware of our prior personal talk. He came into my office, the union waiting to make a strong defense on his behalf stalking the floor in my outer office. He declined union representation knowing what he had been told previously he walked up to my desk, extended his hand, thanked me (for what I don't know), and left my office and the building. The union representatives bolted into my office and demanded I tell them what had happened behind closed doors. They were told the man wished to terminate his services with the Ford Motor Company and did. Their preparation to create a scene and do some in-fighting, without knowing the facts, fell to the floor. All was resolved. The employee was processed off the company rolls as a quit, and was never heard from again. The general foreman was pleased, as I was, and undoubtedly as was the former employee. There were no further peculiar happenings as related to this episode. As an afterthought, he may have kept his trucks in good working order as a result of the parts he had previously stolen.

As it came to pass, I was in one of my favorite clubs late one evening, and Cooper the bartender set me up with a round of drinks, which I had not ordered. There was no one in McMahon's Lounge other than a man in the far corner. I didn't know who he was, but as he raised his glass to me, as he was preparing to leave, I recognized him, and while I have no idea of the number of times he may have been involved stealing, his gesture to me seemed to be an appreciate more toward having treated him in a totally non-personal and dignified manner and I'm sure he was thanking me for that. No words were spoken and left. There is, however, another piece to this little recollection of my past, which I have thought of many times. I saw on more than one occasion contractor trucks with his name on the door panel, leading me to conclude he had gone into the contracting business and from the looks of his equipment, he had done or was doing very well. I apparently did him a big favor by recommending his departure from Ford, and he went on to another way of life.

There were many incidents associated with this era of my learning. As we go along, I'll cite but a few, as overall there were many and too many to ramble on about or recall. During the time I was preparing for one of the many grievance meetings with the union, my office door swung open, as a rather huge black man bolted toward my desk and proceeded to sit in the chair next to me. Something was wrong, and I was grateful he chose to sit down rather than taking a swing at me. He kept mumbling he wasn't well and needed help. Why he came to me I don't know. He swung past the receptionist in my outer office and sat there perspiring like you wouldn't believe. He had a black ebony crucifix around his large neck that he kept rubbing while I was trying to understand what his problem was. The receptionist bolted out of the office and I didn't know where she was heading, other than trying to get out of harm's way. After a few minutes, the phone rang and I answered. The caller was from the security force, asking whether the identified man was in my office. I swung the caller's questions to different subjects so as not to give the big guy notice that he was being tracked out. In short order my office doors again swung open and a couple of burly security men stood over the man in my office. The story had it that they had chased him throughout the warehouse after initially apprehending him in the parking lot of the building as he was hiding parts he had removed from the warehouse. As they took him away and as he kept rubbing his ebony cross, I told the security people to make sure they addressed his concern about being ill. They left and here too was the last I saw of him. Things were happening so fast and I was moving so fast as the many different occasions dictated.

This was the era of the numbers racket, which saw a roaring trade even though it was strictly prohibited by law on the outside and totally outlawed within industry. Gambling on company property, or basically the numbers racket, was looked upon as evil and a negative social influence on those who participated. However, it flourished anyway. The three-penny bet, with an extra penny to box the number (playing your selected number in any sequence) and a possible five-dollar return, was tempting to many. However, it resulted in the loss of one's job if caught, and possible jail time. Compare this to today's society where the lottery and related big-time money games are permitted to exist. It may be hard to fathom that we've come this far from the way it was, but that's how the situation existed not too many decades ago.

I mention this only to bring forth an example that I vividly recall during this period. As previously mentioned, the nature of the work in the parts division and specifically the work assignment of the stock pickers was to locate the bins or assigned storage areas of a stock number appearing on their picking sheets. One had to become accustomed to the numbering series, the related bin locations, and at times even identifying the part by visual observation. There seemed to be a trick in acquiring the job requirements of the classification of stock picker packer checker. I say this only to highlight the confusion that existed at the time in the minds of persons assigned. In an instance that added to the continuing frustrations and confusion to get the job done, it was not uncommon for an individual to write the number he was seeking, beginning with a three-number prefix, for recall purposes, on the side of a carton he may have been working with. This innocent gesture caused one of the employees undue anguish and total embarrassment. As quickly as he jotted the number on the carton, he was at the mercy of a security guard, who, suspecting the worst, cut out that portion of the carton with the number on it, and forcibly directed him off the job without explanation. It seemed as though everyone, including this security guard, was trying to prove to someone above that they were on their toes and doing a good job. Well, stupidity also flourished during this era. The hourly employee was brought into my office, totally confused and trying to explain he was doing his job. It fell on deaf ears. He proceeded to explain that he had placed a part number on a box and the next thing he was being brought into my office for discipline. The security officer proceeded to hand me the piece of carton, removed from the area, identifying it as evidence. He seemed to be overly anxious to get his man and, I suspected, proceeding in his duties without thought. We walked out to the warehouse station, the three of us, as I wanted to see his work order and picking number sequence. The hourly employee properly identified the order number and its corresponding three-number prefix. The same number was written on a piece of the carton the guard brought to my office as evidence. There was no more to say, the employee was told to proceed with his work and I asked the security person to my office. I laid out the circumstances to both him and his supervisor, and requested that he, before proceeding in the future, fully understood the circumstances and acted with some understanding of the implications. I left further discourse, after they left my office, up to the security supervisor. That ended that story, and the security officer's assignment in the warehouse. The experience was another step in my attempt to educate and also create a better relationship between all parties, and to develop understanding of what such negative and hurried actions could cause. The fault was not that of the security guard, but rather that of an era in which such incidents frequently occurred and were met without full understanding of the related facts or the real issue. The instruction seemed to be predicated on problems existing within the Rouge area, and the recourse if you saw anyone acting as though he was involved in the numbers racket, was to apprehend him, and let the labor relations people unravel the situation and dole out the penalty. Unfortunately, I was not making any friends amongst the diehards of the times who measured everything by the notoriety they could accumulate. It seemed the attitude that prevailed was if labor relations voided the action, then it was their fault, not ours.

Shortly before experiencing some of the number incidents encountered, the Rouge complex was having its own problems with the numbers racket. One of the buildings within the complex had been under surveillance for suspected betting. The approach was unto itself quite bold as I recall. The operation was on the rooftop level of one of the Rouge buildings, and those placing bets for themselves and fellow employees regularly lined up each day. Yet the whole time, they were being observed by the Dearborn police. A number of arrests were made on the day of the police raid and followed with complicity and arrests of plant personnel. The arrests by Dearborn police were usually in concert with security management of the company. Each day brought about something different, which was brought to my attention in the security area. Actions like those cited, and the many more impossible to recall, were the setting at the time for many of the requests initiated by security findings and frequently supervisory personnel. More often than not, such actions were an offset to criticism and often times discipline for failure to act. Unfortunately that's the way it was and they too, the security guard and the foreman, had a job to perform. Failure to perform under the frequently valid direction of their supervisors could result in loss of job and family income. Again by today's standards, that way of life was ridiculous and far-fetched in its being.

Ironically, I became well acquainted with several

of the assigned security personnel within the aircraft building. I later learned that the daughter and son-in-law of one of the guards were friends of mine who worked with me in my former Gate 2 employment office days. The other guard was the father of an equally good friend, Chuck Davey, who was then attending Michigan State University and making a name for himself as a major contender in the lightweight boxing arena. Unfortunately, Chuck passed away resulting from an unrelated boxing accident.

Before leaving this era of total confusion, which I believe was resulting from the amalgamation of the many different groups of people the hourly workforce, the salaried employees, the union consolidating their efforts, the supervision trying to maintain a productive workforce, and a newly assembled cadre of supervisors and managers who were desperately trying to be recognized and not certain of the direction they should be taking.

I would like to tell a story of the diverse happenings during this era of two employees, one a cut-up street fighter flaunting his strength, and another who preferred being called the hillbilly, who got into it right in the workplace. From what I understood, a fight had been brewing for some many months of controversy between the two. Supervision in the area was aware of the strong feelings and what was to happen. They kept the situation quiet. It was known that fighting on company property was cause for employee discharge, but even at that, preparation for a fight moved ahead. The fight was on the second floor of the warehouse, conveniently encircled and enclosed by large cartons. The fight, unbeknown to top building management on the first floor and to me, but obviously known by both hourly and supervisory personnel under secret circumstances, took place. When it finally came to my attention, I went into the area to determine how the events took place. No one was talking, either they were away or knew nothing of the circumstances. Hillbilly had beaten the hell out of the bully, blood was all over the place, and the fight had lasted for some time. Rumor had it that he had it coming to him and everyone around accepted the fact. This ended further controversy once and for all between the two of them and all others who had been threatened. Floor supervision and plant security, as well as their subordinates, chose not to talk about what had happened and I wasn't about to probe. Whatever the damage may have been, it was swept under the mat and no one was about to press charges nor make issue of the happening. This again gave credence to the tensions that existed in the workplace between the different types of personalities, brought into the operation from the differing work experiences and backgrounds. I had to live through these situations, and there were many that I could allude to, but for the sake of working toward an ongoing insight of the happenings, unknown to a majority of the people in the company, I'll tell it like it was. Hopefully the youngsters aspiring to break into a workforce such as the one I was a part of will learn that it was no bed of roses. I encountered a similar set of circumstances while in the service. Again, I'll quickly tell you about that, but bypassing some of the more gory details.

A young man, a private first class, who was working for me at the time, had a falling out with the first sergeant of the headquarters company to which we were assigned. Like the episode between the scarred-up bully and the hillbilly, a major fight took place one night on the company street directly adjacent to my quarters. In any event, there was this fight between my guy Chuck and Sergeant Thompson. This, like the other fight in the warehouse, concluded with a lot of blows being struck with blood in the company street, and it carried over to the quarters of the first sergeant. Again blood all over the place, and without the knowledge of the company commander or his aides, all the blood-soaked blankets and clothing were burned by the first sergeant, all night long, in a fifty-gallon barrel, next to the barracks. This was done to eliminate any evidence that a fight had occurred. That which was evident, however, was the dark glasses the first sergeant wore for about a week I understood, because of his eyes being blackened and swollen practically shut, and claiming to those asking questions, that he had been in an accident. Also evident were the badly bruised and swollen hands of Chuck, who had apparently broken more than only his fingers during the fight. Chuck was very loyal to me, insisting that I proceed with my plans for furlough, and wouldn't allow me to take him to the hospital for treatment the next morning, giving me his word he would go to the hospital only after I had departed from camp. We'll not go into greater detail on this piece of background, and if you're really interested and need explanation, write or call me. Now I'll go on with the basic theme of this book.

The purpose of my being hadn't changed. I was in the Ford Motor Company and my sole objective was do what had to be done, whether it be at the hiring line helping those unfortunates get a job and get started in life, or putting out fires in the operation I had become annexed to. Keep in mind I had been sent to this new entity of the company to establish a decentralized employment activity. Instead that which developed and had to be dealt with was a diversified personnel function without lines of demarcation and I was elected to be the overseer. While all the radically differing situations were popping up all around me, and in the midst of total confusion, the company was preparing to make a move of the entire operation to a new and separate location from the Rouge complex. The site plan had been proposed and accepted by the top corporate management. Its location was some fifteen miles away from the Rouge, and a second facility was also proposed for the separation of all Lincoln and Mercury parts and assemblies into another building. This facility was some twelve miles away from the Rouge. Keep in mind both locations were out in the country and access was by dirt road for the most part, with very little development in and around the areas of the proposed sites. This was far away. I've already taken you through some of the happenings that took place at the new location and hopefully you will track out with me as I jump back and forth between the aircraft building at the Rouge complex and the new location. Please stay with me, it'll all fall in place.

The question of the union representation and jurisdictional alignment, while explicitly spelled out in the wording of the main agreement between company and union, seemed to be a case of wasted verbiage when it came down to actual practice. This seemed to be just another case of making an existing situation fit the need, rather than the adherence to that recognized and supposedly understood by the rank and file. The area for the new locations fell properly within the union representation authority of the outlying company structured locations, and that's the way it should have been. Not so politics and pressures again entered the picture, and the union group who had established themselves quite firmly in the minds of the union upper echelons, by a flick of a finger convinced company labor relations management that it was their option to stay or move to the new location with representational jurisdiction on their side. Not realistically so, the basic contract between the parties spoke differently. In the meantime the outlying union structure was devoid of any question pertaining to their authority in the matter, and again, absent any logical matter, politics intervened and the strength of the table-pounders won over without convincing argument or rationale. The union's representation structure responsible for other than the metropolitan area was apparently fast asleep and the strong arm of the controlling group automatically called the shots and made themselves comfortable in their new arena.

It once again seemed useless to force a position that the situation should have been properly examined, with all parties sharing in the conclusion, but once again it was a more matter of clout and less a proper interpretation of the related facts. My strong feelings were that the outlying local union had proper jurisdiction and should have made a case for their benefit. Unfortunately this never happened. In the meantime those in power cordoned off jurisdictional authority and forced themselves into positions of authority. The greater piece of the pie included a separate representational alignment for the Lincoln Mercury spin-off, again making a good thing even better for the group with the necessary clout. In retrospect, jurisdictional assignment, where it was to properly fall would have saved countless hours of bickering at the new location, and thousands of dollars, not to mention satisfying the countless grievances being filled each day. The union had a good thing going and they knew it. The fault for allowing this poorly conceived relationship to flourish, in my opinion, fell squarely in the lap of the then top level labor relations people of the company, again unwilling to intervene properly, but rather conceding and taking the easy way out.

While the union's representation structure was defined for purposes of the new facilities, the question of the hourly workforce was still in limbo. The resultant conclusions included a mixture of considerations. For example, there were those willing to continue on their jobs and transfer to the new locations. I had to work out agreements with the union to ensure their interests were met. There were others in our midst who, because of the distance factor, wanted no part of the move and sought placement within the total Rouge complex. This too had to be worked out by agreement and concurrence of upper levels of the company and union. On the other hand, there were employees now working within the Rouge complex requesting consideration for transfer to the new location, some even willing to sacrifice their total in-plant seniority for a fresh start at the new locations. This gives you some idea of the heartaches and the trauma arising from the proposed new operation, and in this case the first such gigantic operation and people move ever undertaken by the company within the metropolitan area, and again I was in the middle of this hodge-podge trying to keep the pieces together, while the operation continued without missing a beat. The profits were too great to do otherwise. The new site was purchased, I understand, from two brothers who owned the property and the payout made them wealthy, allowing them to carry through with their wishes for a move to the West Coast. It didn't take long for building construction to begin and in short order there appeared a long trail of trucks, trailers, cabs, and any other vehicles to transport stock from the two-story aircraft building in the Rouge complex, to the new and huge one-story warehouse location far out in the suburbs. At the time, that's what it was referred to by most, as going out to the suburbs, and much thought was going into accepting a job transfer. One of the things that caused considerable confusion was a system by which employees could be identified as to where they fit in the arena of employment. There was need to separate employees coming into the new facility, regardless of where they had been within the company, from those regularly assigned. To put the dilemma to rest, I suggested a badge designation with the letter "M" (for Move) identifying the newcomers to the operation and when all settled down, it would be a simple thing to separate those to be returned to their basic locations, creating no injustice to those having tenure in the operation. The idea took hold and everyone was quite happy with the concept.

My responsibilities included having enough working and on-hand personnel to phase out the Rouge aircraft operation, as well as providing enough staffing to receive incoming huge quantities of stock at the new location. My duties were not on an eight-hour-a-day basis but rather moving between locations at all hours day or night as the move took place. Roller skates, bicycles, or the like would have served well to assist in getting from one area to another within the new location. It was huge and very difficult to identify individuals in the far reaches of the facility. I recall more than once whistling or calling a person by name that was off in the distance, and then waiting until the sound of my calling got back. The new warehouse was, as I've said before, large, and with the caravan of trucks bringing in tons of stock, unloading all day and night, and warehouse people unloading and finding proper locations, it was slowly beginning to fill. The same type of activity was going on simultaneously with the location identified for Lincoln and Mercury parts, a separate parts depot facility located on Telegraph Road, also in Livonia, Michigan. Ours was to ship the materials to the location, and they in turn with their separate management took on the responsibility from there.

We had by this time identified our organization staffing and hired many hourly and salaried employees for the new location, including many former policemen, retired security personnel, and the like. My recollection identified about thirty newly hired security persons within the larger of the locations. They were trained people, mostly from the small communities near the new facility. I found them to be considerate, willing to understand what their required duties were to be, and above all, they were courteous in their dealings with the employees. Apart from all the accolades, they were appreciative of obtaining employment with the company at the new location, and with a salary income considerably above that which they had been accustomed to. We were settling in on both our staffing needs as well as our operational requirements and starting up a new but difficult facility for the Ford Motor Company.

It was at this time that the man I was responsible to came to my office on one of his infrequent visits and informed me he had been fired. As I previously told you, I would inform you of this piece of the story in our subsequent chapters, and this is it. His attitude was quite jovial, and without the display of expected remorse, he asked me to join him for lunch. I recall telling him I wasn't in the mood for jesting on an important issue as job loss and I didn't believe him, and further, was too busy to play games. We eventually did go to lunch together, where much to my surprise, his story was pieced together. It seemed there had been more than one source reporting to his superiors of their dissatisfaction with his performance and they wanted him out. His termination would not affect me nor the people working for me, even though we, by organizational alignment, had supposedly functioned under his jurisdiction. It was just a matter of time and the Montgomery Ward people, his superiors, finally awakened to their responsibilities. The actions were fierce. He could have been given the benefit of a lesser assignment within the organization that in fact originally had selected him. Ironically, the information that he was passing on to me seemed to affect me more than it did him. I was hard pressed to accept the totality of the rationale while he seemed composed and disenchanted with what had occurred. His only path of survival seemed to be a return to the staff activity that had acquiesced in his original transfer. He was fortunate in finding a friend who was willing to accept him in a plant operation capacity, and from there through his appeals, and a considerable time lapse, he was properly returned to the activity that had dismissed him. He was eventually placed in an assignment, which, rather than resorting to dismissal, was favorable for him. He was transferred to the Seattle depot field location. Before he left the metropolitan area, he told me that he and his family were pleased with his new area of residence and new line of work. He was assigned to our Seattle location as a floor supervisor. He visited me at work and also at my home some several years later and we spoke of the various office experiences as well as my wife's and my wedding, which he and his family had attended and remembered very well. He seemed quite content with life. I was grateful for the confidence he initially bestowed on me and for his original support for assignment to what turned out to be a career path until I retired some forty-two years later. He could have been a different and better person had he better considered the dilemma he had created for himself as well as me in our combined period of life.

Again, getting back to the original theme of this book, and as a part of one of the job reviews, I accompanied one of the guards as he made his rounds at the new location. It was during this walkthrough that we kept hearing from nowhere a voice calling for help. We looked all around and finally concluded the voice was that of a youngster, and the sound was coming from a manhole cover in the floor. We tracked this down through the building and out the far side, abutting what was known as the turkey farm. By this time we were both in a ditch in water up to our knees. A youngster was in a drain and because of the heavy fencing at the far end, he was unable to get out. We finally dug away at the siding and he was able to crawl out. He was about ten or twelve years of age and told us he had walked beneath the surface starting at the GM building, approximately three blocks away. He was not aware that a flash flood could have caused him to drown, as he had no exit. He was quite content to get out of the drain, and walked away quite happily. This near tragedy set in motion the immediate need for a sewer fencing arrangement at the property entrance, something that should have been done but was not. When I called this to upper management's attention, they couldn't understand how it happened, but did understand the importance for immediate action and installed a temporary barrier at the entrance of the sewer pipe until the proper engineering fixture was in place. In the meantime, I contacted the adjacent GM facility apprising them of the situation and recommended strongly that they block off the entry, thereby preventing a recurrence of what could have been a major tragedy. They fully understood the implications and indicated handling was essential and they would immediately respond.

CHAPTER 24
IDENTIFIED CONSTRUCTION SHORTCOMINGS

While we're on the subject of unreported incidents that could have easily led to loss of life or major tragedy, I'll tell you about another shortcoming on the part of those responsible for building construction. Sometime after occupancy of the building, a major drinking water incident occurred. It seemed the intake standup pipes, gasoline, water, chemicals, etc. were not properly marked, or not identified at all. By complete mistake, and without seeking advice, the gasoline delivery of some twenty thousand gallons of gasoline was inadvertently connected to the water intake rather than the gasoline retention tanks and as a consequence flowed underground throughout the building and up to the drinking fountains of the building. Fortunately, the mistake was immediately discovered by the security personnel and they in turn set needed corrective actions in motion. All fountains were secured, as were the manhole covers in the building. A cigarette inadvertently dropped in a manhole could have easily ignited and caused incalculable building and people loss. Fortunately, the incident was discovered late in the day with but a few people in the building. Security people began the task of flushing out the system of the gasoline. Thousands of gallons of water were used to cleanse the system. The process lasted all weekend long. By the following Monday, with hundreds of people working lots of man-hours to ensure safety, all was reported back to normal. Again the building construction people and engineers were at a loss as to the mis-designation or non-identification of the intake system. This too was corrected immediately, and fortunately without incident or loss.

My walk around the premises, both indoors and out, in the company of the security guard, led me to the outside large open acreage in the rear of the building. By the way this open area has since been built over, and provides a facility twice the size of the original building concept. During our walk, we inadvertently flushed several beautiful pheasants from their nesting locations. I learned sometime later that the routing that we had traveled was by no means accidental but rather by design, as it frequently provided a catch for the guard and a healthy meal for his family. As I mentioned before, most of the new security force was from the surrounding farm community and it was not uncommon for them to occasionally go hunting, fishing, or otherwise to provide food for the table.

Throughout this period of mass confusion in attempting to launch a productive operation, the union persisted in presenting numerous grievances, most of which were of little or no significance and, more frequently than not, were identified with floor supervisors performing work the union felt to be that of an hourly employee. It was difficult to keep everyone in line, when in fact there were no lines of job demarcation. Most of the activity was in a stage of flux and uncertainty, and for all purposes, much was being done by trial and error. Unfortunately, the position of the local union representatives was to put it in writing and let the management respond. As a consequence, the grievance workload literally rolled up in my office. The times were difficult to contend with. In a particular controversy, after arguing the issues for the better part of the day, I couldn't make further inroads toward settling the issues.

There was considerable money at stake and the union was in the catbird's seat. They wouldn't negotiate on the real issues and held me hostage for settlement with pay to a number of aggrieved listed employees, none of whom knew the issue involved, but as a class action merely endorsed what had been initiated. Mike, the union chairman, was dictating his personal and totally prejudicial position to his subordinates and insisting, as union chairman, they follow his lead. I was getting nowhere with him and his total blocking of cooperation, negotiations, or logic.

While I had the authority to resolve the grievance by monetary settlement, I was doubly hard-pressed to abdicate principal. I knew I had to be resourceful in my approach for a settlement in that the union spokesman was not only challenging in his demeanor but demanding a payoff. I knew something of his background and his affiliation with a club membership where he was held high as the champion morra player in his large Italian surroundings and club associates. The game of morra, if you hadn't heard of it or played the game, is something like scissors, stone, and paper, but much more fierce in its delivery and outcome. You play for points, and two, four, or six players is usually the pairing off. The losers pay for a round of drinks, or whatever is at stake, and challengers are invited in for the subsequent rounds. To give you some idea of how vocal and fierce this game can become, I was told that in Italy it has been outlawed, because more often than not, because of the associated liquor fights can erupt and someone can get hurt.

I challenged Mike to a three-point match. Winner takes all. I knew something about the game and its pitfalls. I had learned the game well as a partner to my father who was an expert. Mike's associates asked to talk to me privately, which I agreed to. They tried to caution me in promoting this course of action, as they and their peers knew of Mike's strength in this game of morra. If you'd like to know more about the game contact me and I'll be glad to give you some pointers. We entered my conference room enclosed in cinder, block walls, understanding if I lost there would be a monetary resolve at stake, while if on the other hand I won, all of the grievances relating to the issue would be summarily removed from the docket and without question. Mike's closest companion, Jake, was in the room and paced nervously. The game was set for three points and accordingly began across the large conference table. The game is played by loud number calling, in addition and simultaneously there is a showing of a number of fingers on one hand, as I said before, something like the game of rock, scissors, and paper. Loud is putting it mildly, shouting is more like it, I wasn't sure of his approach to the game, never having seen him play or knowing his strengths or weaknesses. I won the first point, got a feel for my opponent's strategy, and won the next two points for game. All of the grievances were gathered up and a quiet exit by Mike and his compatriot followed. I said nothing further, and it was some several weeks later that Jake told me in confidence that Mike never got over the total defeat, and would be careful in the future as to who he accepted a challenge from. In the meantime, Jake informed me that he had been sworn to secrecy about Mike's loss amongst his peers as well as his east side club associates. My method of effectively resolving the grievances was not within the prescribed way of doing business and if the results had surfaced in a negative atmosphere to my well-being, I'm sure I could have been condemned or crucified. You have no idea of how critical it was to get a resolution to the ridiculous hard-headed position that Mike had taken. All the employees endorsing the grievance action as professed by the union chairman were never heard from. The abolition of the issue with his constituency was for Mike to resolve.

It was not uncommon for me to arrive on the job early and do research and investigation into the late hours in trying to stay abreast of the issues and be able to respond with some intelligence as the items were brought for review and discussion. It was a tough time for me and it appeared I was getting hit from all angles in an attempt to do a commendable job for the company as well as myself. Chrysler made me a big offer about this time, and for the love of God I'll never understand why I just didn't drop the mess I had to deal with daily and join them under a different banner. Conversely, I had been asked to oversee a program for a building dedication. This was in the mid-1950s. Letters of invitation to the Ford executives, the press, and the city fathers had to be initiated. Included were the speeches I had to prepare, and one in particular was a presentation speech I prepared for the manager of the facility. He really didn't know what was going on, or what was expected of him, as they'd never done anything so grandiose at Montgomery Ward where he had come from. I enjoyed doing this for him, and watched him reciting my words as he very nervously made the presentation in the midst of several hundred employees, with major company executives who had been invited, and, as customary, with the Fords in attendance.

On more than one occasion, in my efforts to calm him down, I informed him I had aligned the Fords as to their role and responsibilities and they appeared ready to take the stage.

My wife had purchased a movie camera as a gift for me. While new for the times, it and I were limited in our photographic abilities, capturing only some of the happenings of the event. That which I still have is a limited view of Henry and Benson Ford coming onto the scene for the building dedication. William Clay was not with us at that time. He may have been going to school or on business elsewhere. I might add that while the building manager was nervous, the Fords were no exception they seemed more nervous than George, the building manager. They followed my instructions to a tee and were very complimentary when the whole thing was concluded. The policy of the company dictated a building dedication was an appropriate consideration to undertake. I, for one, felt the public relations people, especially with all the dignitaries from the community being invited, let alone the Fords being there, could have had a field day. Why me?

During this traumatic period in my career, my youngest sister Bernice was in the process of being interviewed with Ford for assignment in the administration level in the company's executive offices. Her placement in the office of John Bugas, the vice president, pleased me greatly, and her orientation was in the area I was familiar with. Like me, she was privy to situations that existed and the passing scene. The other members of the family were also fortunate in their career paths, as both Irene and Marian carved out positions in office administration at the higher levels of locally respectable organizations. In the meantime assistance was there also for my dad, who had been with Ford many years, merely trudging ahead day by day. I was ultimately successful in having him removed from a factory environment in a semi-skilled job, and given an assignment in building maintenance in the main office building. The wages were considerably less, but his attitude was, "Why couldn't I have gotten this assignment years ago?"

The family pulled together, and while history was being made, for us it was a happy time. While we're talking family, my friend Marge and I became engaged and shortly thereafter, after her final university classes, she became my wife, and a school teacher. I had been going to school during this entire dilemma, trying to complete an education while confronted with all sorts of work-related roadblocks. In the meantime, the company selected me to participate in their newly developed industrial management educational programs, four years of study four nights a week and four hours a night. I accepted the offer, dropped out of my university classes temporarily during this period and put up with the added grief until graduation. It was during this period we had Punky, Teresa Lynn, who made my life then as well as now very complete and meaningful. Today we have Rick, Teresa's husband, and four grandchildren, all of whom are a big part of our family, with Nick, the oldest, excelling in baseball, his sister Danielle with high academic standings and competing in sports, her sister Alyssa also competing in gymnastics, and Jaymie, a twin, professing to be the greatest noodle connoisseur.

CHAPTER 25
THE KOREAN WAR STOPS
NEW CONSTRUCTION

T hings began to happen in a big way about this time. We were beginning to settle down in our new environment, but like previous times, nothing proper seemed to last very long. While the plans of the company called for another new building for the multitude of engineers associated with this newly formed entity of the business, a new building was not to happen. The Korean War effort took precedent, and a major move into a new location requiring brick and mortar and iron and steel was set aside. Instead, arrangements had to be made to house the hundreds of people who had lost their quarters resulting from all the moves and locations involved. The newly constructed building we were in was selected as the site, until other arrangements could be made at some future time.

Construction of revamped office facilities was immediately begun, encroaching on several bays of the large warehouse. Phone lines dangled from the ceiling to each of the desks below, and where this couldn't accommodate the need, lines were strung out on the floor with plastic covering to avoid the tripping hazards. Executive offices were put in place, the cafeteria was enlarged to twice its normal size, parking lot rearrangement was necessary, new servicing personnel were added, as were adequate restrooms to meet the new needs. We had gone through this most recently in the initial phases of building occupancy, and here we were at it again. This on again, off again, seemed to be a way of life in the group I was affiliated with and for better or worse, I was stuck with it. And until I had served my time or was fortunate enough to be selected for another way of work and life, my personal dictates held me steadfast to doing a good job with hope that better things had to happen. They did.

Before leaving this theatre of many happenings, there is one more thing that needs mentioning and perhaps should have followed that portion of this book that dealt with Mr. Ford's personal involvement in helping others. I'm talking of Mr. Ford, the first. He personally adopted a school of youngsters located in New England area. He was fond of the area and traveled most of the countryside, let alone the area, and the restoration he was identified with. The young boys Ford sponsored ultimately became employees of the company, many of whom earned their income working in the various company cafeterias, and becoming managers, dining room chefs, and the like. They were under the guidance of Mr. Ford and responsible for working and finding their way through life. We had the benefit of several of these youngsters working in our facilities. Their abilities had been well tested and tried long before joining us as they somewhat automatically fell in line with our need and never missed a beat. I was fortunate to have become acquainted with several of these now young men, and one couldn't meet a more polite and people-oriented type of individual. Also on the payroll was a young man who had a story to tell. Unlike Mr. Ford's helping hand, this man's existence within the company was a cover-up to a deal that had apparently been cut by the Detroit Police Department and the Harry Bennett regime, if not by Harry Bennett himself. The story may sound far reaching, but having become fairly well acquainted with the young man, in fact, does bring it into play many of the circumstances realistic to Tony's portrayal of his tragedy.

Tony was a product of the lower east side of Detroit where crime ran rampant and employment was scarce during and after the Depression. As a youngster playing in the neighborhood back alleys, he was shot by a police officer mistaking him for another. He tells of being left to die in the alley. As a policeman crouched over him, he wrestled the gun away from him and apparently killed him. While Tony was recovering from the gunshot wound and the resultant seizures and partial mobility, his family was offered, in exchange for their total repression of the unfortunate episode, a lifetime job at the Ford Motor Company as a payoff. They accepted. It is again important to understand that a job, particularly at Ford, was tantamount to a life ticket to future security and continuing wealth. The dates and residence location were still fresh in Tony's mind when he unraveled the tale to me, in fact on more than one occasion. Unfortunately, nothing in his personnel record substantiated a reason for his placement in the Ford Motor Company. His exacting recall of the happenings, and names which he professed to having been involved in his job with the company, all tied together with his employment. There was, however, no recorded evidence in his personnel jacket, the original copy of which I had in my files. That which he had in his favor was the fact he was incapacitated and was given a job, something that was not done routinely, and in this instance, giving credence to this tale of woe. Additionally, an endorsement by those sponsoring his acceptance in his totally incapacitated condition was obviously swept under the rug, as it appeared nowhere in the record.

I became involved with Tony's employment, as he was physically handicapped and difficult to keep employed. In that every person's responsibility was well-documented and measured against budget completion, he couldn't keep up with his assignments according to his supervision and as such he was considered a budget liability in the area to which he was assigned. Unlike the attitude which prevailed during Mr. Ford's tenure for handicapped personnel, no allowances existed during this period of the budget and performance race. While Tony's recall of the happenings leading to his disfigurement and major handicap fit well into the happenings of the times, i.e., the underworld activities, the bravado of the police organization, the *mano a mano* relationships existing between the police, the security at Ford, and the Bennett regime, the actual supporting evidence did not exist. His reason for being, with reliance on written evidence, was apparently long-before suppressed, conveniently disposed of, and forgotten. The existent in record identification form was not supportable nor alluded to. This I knew, as I had thoroughly reviewed the record. That which I personally could relate to and recall was the happenings of the times, and could understand the gullibility of a despondent Italian family who envisioned total reward for the misfortune that had befallen one of their sons.

On more than one occasion his removal from assigned employment tasks was called to my attention and in each instance I stalled the action. I personally spoke with him several times alerting him of the inevitable if he wouldn't heed the demands of his supervision. They would, in the society of the times, succeed in getting him out. I carried the concern further by talking to his wife, who at the time was also with Ford. She reaffirmed to me chapter and verse Tony's handicap and story surrounding it. He tried to understand but it was apparent the direction wouldn't hold. Ultimately my recommendation for some semblance of performance and retention was a janitorial assignment for Tony within the medical offices. This would protect him from the barbs of supervision and at the same time provide a safe haven in the event of his seizures. He was given a fresh white uniform daily and a black bow tie. I made it a point to observe him as I passed through the medical facilities on future occasions and often times observed his other-than-proper appearance. I would privately give him a polite dressing down for being unkempt, not shaving, and not wearing his bow tie. He understood my reprimand and for the next few days tried his best to look the part. Tony never took exception to my direction and inwardly knew the helping hand I was extending. This appreciation came to the forefront when my wife and I were invited to his son's large wedding, again on the east side of Detroit and with what appeared to be many Mafioso attendees. I was happy for him and his family as they and Tony, even with his severe handicap, were able to celebrate the festivities of the evening.

CHAPTER 26
PROMOTION AND NEW RESPONSIBILITIES

It finally happened; around this period. I was removed from my assignment as what was to have been an employment manager and never was, and, promoted to division responsibility overseeing field activities in both the salaried personnel and hourly union relationships. It happened so fast that my new immediate manager was not even involved, but rather was told I was to be transferred. Sometimes good things happen in your career path that you know nothing of or control. I lost track of Tony after that, but felt I had positioned him properly and with the slightest assistance he could carry on. Again for anyone reading my account of happenings, I was grateful that I had tried hard to succeed over the years and this was the payoff. It didn't come easy, and for those of you interested, it never will.

There were eighteen locations nationwide to the activity that I was assigned to, each with their own management controls, union representation, and problem issues. Apart from my normal assignment experiences I was also given the responsibility of security at our field locations and safety, as I was acquainted with the requirements and had some experience in handling that end of the ledger as well. I was given the opportunity to visit the locations right from the beginning of my new appointment. With mild exception, the problems cited during my review were absolutely minimal. The hard-bitten attitudes which existed with the seasoned Detroit union representation were in fact non-existent in the field locations. The standards for security and safety were also in place and being handled effectively.

For all intents, there was solidarity in the relationship between management and the local union. Their objectives were understood and the employees, salaried and hourly, strove to meet the requirements. It was a beautiful thing to see, and I was lucky enough to see and understand a good thing which I was now responsible to oversee. Very little direction was necessary, and for the most part I had gone through the experiences cited as problems, and based on my experiences, I assisted the assigned personnel and carried them through what they felt to be insurmountable issues. I was invited to attend the union meetings and to discuss with them solutions within the framework of the national union contract, responding to the issues. They were concerned, long-service, and conscientious employees. I didn't realize the transformation that existed between my Detroit union experience and that which I was experiencing at our field locations. My life would have been much more pleasant had I been initially assigned to one of these corners of heaven, but unfortunately, my destiny was to prove my worth, starting at the other end.

Having the new responsibilities, it seemed that

anything of a problem nature with people at our out-lying eighteen locations was directed to my attention. I accepted the role, as with the background I fortunately had accumulated, and as I said before, the issues were not difficult to cope with. The people at our Memphis location never did get their "black only" drinking fountains or restrooms signs back. The story behind this now-it-can-be-told episode relates to a phone call I received from one of the executive offices telling me get rid of the signs. There was no discourse as to how this was to be done, nor of the explosive controversial nature of things at the location and the southern loca-tions in general. I was ordered to get it done by one of our hiding executives. That's all I needed and felt I had been given a green flag.

I gathered the management of the location together and instructed them to go out and make a purchase of paint, sufficiently large to paint the whole warehouse and adjacent facilities, and if there were questions, direct them to me. The painting and spraying began, even though it had been completed some two years earlier, and a twenty-year time lag would not have been uncommon. The instruction was to paint over the "black only" signs and forget to repaint them. The "blacks only" drinking fountains were to have their plumbing disconnected during this refurbishing, and not reconnected. The task was accomplished and everyone at the location was pleased with the new look and effort. Not a thing was said about the removal of the signs during or since then. A good thing was done for the people of the Memphis Depot; they were proud and I was pleased with our accomplishments. A little ingenuity went a long way and not a word was uttered by my budget-crazed executive who had ordered me to get the job done. It was done. I received no thanks for having done the impossible. I learned to understand and accepted this way of straight-line management and subordinate relationships. I also learned later that the assigner was receiving all the accolades for a job well done, and I really didn't care. By the way, young readers, that's another thing you learn in this vicious society: the man ahead of you will frequently get the rewards, whether deserving or not, and frequently and unfortunately at your expense. Grin and bear it, your day will come.

Elvis was there, yes Elvis Presley. He came into the administrative front side of the building and walked through the lobby to the first open office he saw. I recall, after an interesting and friendly greeting, I directed him to the building manager's office. Aureen, the executive secretary, detected someone standing next to her trying to get her attention by clearing his throat. She looked up and saw this big handsome man next to her desk. Aureen's comment to me was with two sons attending the ministry, "I was blushing and completely overwhelmed by his presence. I'm sure," she said, "I reacted like a giddy teenage stage-struck follower. He was a perfect gentleman and seemed to understand my dilemma and proceeded slowly to tell me what he wanted. He repeated his request twice, to ensure I understood. He wanted to place an order for two fully-equipped white Lincolns." He told Aureen he had driven by the location many times and thought it best to handle his request personally. He went on to say he was making a present of the vehicles to two of his friends and asked the cars be either delivered to his residence, Graceland, a short driving distance from our distribution center, or he would make arrangements for pick-up. Aureen tells the story that after regaining her composure and knowing well he was in the wrong area for the car order, she asked him to accompany her to our sales department down the hall from where she was located. He obliged her, and together they walked down to the sales manager's office. "Can you for a minute imagine," Aureen was saying, "Elvis Presley and I walking down the corridor together, carrying on a conversation like old friends as we were walking. The word had gotten around that Elvis was in the building, and as curiosity and disbelief mounted, my acquaintances from office to office, as we walked, conveniently found their way to the doorways and the corridors just to get a peek. It was understandable."

Elvis Presley received delivery of his two Lincolns at Graceland in record-breaking time. Aureen, I'm sure, has repeated this story many times over to all of her family and friends. This had to be the highlight of her career with Ford and it couldn't have happened to a nicer and more perfect lady. Unfortunately, I missed talking to Elvis at great length as I was deeply involved in the forward movement of the painting that was taking place. My short meeting with Elvis Presley was, and has been, a most moving experience for me. I did make it a point to drive in front of beautiful Graceland on my way back to my hotel that evening and saw the beautifully scrolled ironwork in the form of lavender musical notes encircling his estate. The next day Aureen, still very excited, told me the story all over again.

Before bringing the many and pleasurable happenings that I was fortunate to have experienced and frequently been a part of, I reluctantly must also inform you of the demise of the Ford shipping fleet. The article written by Bob Kreipke, Corporate Historian of the Ford World Newspaper of the company (copy attached), titled "Ford freighters ride waves of history," captures the true meaning, history, and beauty of the Henry, Benson, and Clay as well as other ships identified as part of the Ford fleet.

Like the many memorable experiences of the past, my association with the ships, their officers and crew leaves me with great remorse on learning of this passing of history. I'm sure this feeling is shared by the many who had come to know the ships, the beauty of having been there, and this era of the past.

My new position entailed considerable travel, from the East Coast locations to the west, north, and south. I had just about completed my reviews with the manager of our New Orleans distribution center when I received a call to route my return via St. Louis. Our central Ford offices had been alerted to the fact that a new stock dis-

HISTORICALLY SPEAKING

Ford freighters ride waves of history

BY BOB KREIPKE
Corporate Historian

December can be a time of transition into deep winter, especially if you are a sailor on the Great Lakes. Jr is hard to imagine that a company producing vehicles for getting around on land would also successfully run a large fleet

of ships, but that's what Ford Motor Company did for more than 50 years.

Henry Ford was familiar with ships, having worked early on at the Detroit Dry Dock Company helping construct ships. During World War 1, Ford bid on and received a large U.S. government contract to build submarine chaser boats for the Navy.

As part of the deal, the government agreed to help develop property by the Rouge River. This included a canal allowing the finished ships to sail out from the Rouge property. The shipbuilding project was short-lived because, fortunately, the war came to

an end. That was not the end of Ford's interest in shipping, however.

In 1923, Ford ordered two custom-built ships for transporting raw materials to the new Rouge steel operation. These ships were to be the maximum 600-foot length that could just fit through the Soo Locks in Sault Ste. Marie, Michigan, enabling them to sail into Lake Superior.

Both of these vessels would be the most modern freighters on the Great Lakes. The ships were powered by diesel engines instead of coal. With huge longstroke, four-cylinder engines, they were designed for longtime, dependable service.

The engines themselves were designed to run quietly, but the sound the exhaust made could be heard for miles. Henry Ford once commented that the rhythmic exhaust sounded like someone saving "making money, making money, making money."

The ships were named the Henry Ford II and the Benson Ford and were launched in the spring of 1924. There were no ordinary cargo ships. Much of

the hardware was chrome plated and redone every year. The ships were the first on the Great Lakes to utilize electricity to operate the winches and steering gears. Other vessels used steam to power their equipment. Electricity also was utilized in the kitchen. In the 1950s and 1960s, Ford added several more vessels - the William Clay Ford, the John Dykstra, the Robert McNamara and the Ernest Breech.

Unfortunately, by the early 1980s, American steel production had diminished as foreign markets expanded their production and exports. As a result, Ford reorganized the Rouge Steel operation as a subsidiary. By this time, shipping costs also were getting expensive, and Ford's fleet of ships was aging and in need of construction maintenance.

The Benson Ford was scrapped in 1983. The pilothouse was put on South Bass Island in Lake Erie. The William Clay Ford was scrapped in 1984, and its pilothouse was placed at the Dossin Great Lakes Museum in Detroit. In 1989, Ford sold the majority of Rouge Steel operations, including three of the remaining three vessels. The Henry Fords II sat dormant for

several years in a Toledo, Ohio, harbor, and then was towed to Canada in late 1994 and cut up into scrap metal.

A glorious era had come to an end. The Ford fleet was a magnificent sight to watch, especially as it navigated down at the Detroit River or along the Great Lakes shipping lanes. These symbols of strength and independence will be fondly remembered.

patch center had been opened by the parts and service management, again without receiving proper clearances, and hell-bent on election, they were going to do it their way. Again the approach smacked of the aloof and independent way Montgomery Ward conducted business. For all their purposes, they visualized a better way to service the St. Louis dealers with quicker delivery schedule and more profitable handling.

Here we go again. By the time I arrived, it was apparent the planning for this operation was well underway, Ford stock was neatly arranged in rows the length of the building, employees were already hired as was their supervision, and the most surprising thing to me was the lineup of local cabs, not trucks, but taxicabs awaiting their call for parts delivery. I quickly beckoned the manager, a young industrial engineer, and asked him under what and whose authority he was acting. Being somewhat headstrong, his response centered on how this was a good thing for Ford and he'd been given the green light to proceed. This is where the big mistake occurred — it wasn't the young engineer's fault, but rather that of his next-in-line superior who signed off on the proposal. Once the experiment had been tested, the plan was to expand the concept to several other critical delivery points of the country. What I was hearing was that he had an opportunity, and would run with it for all it was worth. A nicer guy would be hard to come by, but unfortunately he missed his calling within the strict and solidified structure of the company. A line and staff organizational structure dictated presentation and acceptance by the next staff operation with responsibility in the area of endeavor. None of this had been done. He saw stars and a great opportunity and proceeded without getting the right approvals. Apart from the many quick violations I witnessed just by my first glance, he had commissioned the Teamsters Union taxicab drivers, a direct violation of our existing operating agreement by contract with the UAW.

I told him right out, cancel all agreements initiated, provide severance pay and termination to those hired, get the Ford stock back to its rightful location, and inform the Teamsters that the experiment had concluded. I further informed him I would be in the city for the next few days and expected compliance with my instruction. If he had questions, I would be glad to hear any complaints in his manager's office back at our headquarters, as I planned to ensure that his superiors also fully understood the direction. During the next few days, his dream operation was grinding down to a halt. I left the city, confident that the message had gotten through.

To my surprise, by the time I returned to our offices, I learned that he had already been there and was appealing his position to his management. As I said before, he was a friend, and I would have expected otherwise, but no, he decided his course of action was the best for him, and was hoping I would be berated for having taken such strong measures against the plans. Keep in mind I had apprised him of what I had to do as a result of my findings and the dictates handed down from our central offices. It fell on deaf ears. His management never said a thing to me nor questioned the decision. The experiment was destined to fall apart, and it did. No further experimental centers were considered. Whether my headstrong friend really understood the rationale accompanying my direction to him, I don't know, but I do know his management proceeded with caution and clearance before undertaking future unplowed terrain. Their checks and balances with me and other authority was a measure of adjustment for them and rightful progress.

As I traveled from one field location to another, not only did I become acquainted with the respective operations, but I began to understand some of the attitudes and desires of the employees. They felt comfortable in confiding to me some of their ambitions and long-range desires with the company. In certain cases I was able to assist in their requested upgrading within the location, making adjustments in their assignments, and in a few instances reassigning the individuals to promotional or lateral assignment at other company locations. With the exception of the travel and long periods of absence from my family, I enjoyed what I was doing, was well received, and enjoyed working with our field locations.

The work was varied in its nature, and in that I became known as their answer man, I was in constant touch with their management, and in most instances directly communicating with the concerned employees. As you may recall, I emphasized earlier in this writing that the employees for the most part were long-service personnel. They were proud to be associated with Ford and had the opportunity to enjoy the benefits, particularly the opportunity to live a comfortable life and raise a good and educated family by way of the income received. They, as employees, were not the college-oriented type. When they began work, for the most part, employment was hard to come by and once employed, they applied themselves conscientiously and proudly. The income level was established at the Ford staff offices, it was applied across all locations of the company and all employees. It was recognized they were being paid a much higher dollar than customarily paid in their geographic locations. They were proud of their association with Ford and it showed.

CHAPTER 27
LEE IACOCCA STOPS THE END RUN

I became aware of something that was obviously of concern at a particular time, and was as much a bother to a number of the salaried and management employees at a number of locations as it was to me. Several managers contacted me confidentially wanting to better understand the meaning of a questionnaire sent to their employees dealing basically with their backgrounds, including education, requests for colleges attended, years of attendance, and dates of graduation. The questionnaire was requesting response to several areas of concern, under the guise of updating the personnel records of all employees. Its main focus was, however, on education, and that was not difficult to see through. While the inquiries centered on "what was this all about," those asking didn't want it to appear they were questioning the authority of the request, nor did they want to find themselves in a position of being less than good soldiers in following instruction. Their concerns and that of the employees were centered on being replaced on their jobs that they had worked so hard to achieve, or displaced because of a lack of a degree or formal education. They came to me.

I was able to get, in short order, a copy of the executive questionnaire directly from one of our field locations. It was as they said, slanted toward education, and why? Information copies were restricted in their distribution by the writer, as though related publicity may have been detrimental to getting the project started and completed. We obviously had around us a lot of headstrong individuals who intended to develop some data from the information expected as a response. Again as in another cited case, we needed to tighten up the screws. No in-line approvals had been received for the release of the questionnaire. Instructions were communicated without regard to corporate approval, nor of superior review and approvals. It was again a time for some ambitious executive to blindly latch on to a star, and in the exuberance of the moment, seek recognition for an initiated and completed work effort. Well, fortunately he didn't get very far as a consequence of my becoming involved and understand what was going on in the minds of the field management employees.

Their thoughts of being demoted or completely eliminated because of a lack of a formal education were obvious and of major concern. Their questions revolved around whether they had done something wrong, and how about the many years of acceptable work they'd been performing for Ford. These mixed emotions and thoughts were disrupting and surfacing throughout our field locations. I cautioned everyone raising the question to stand by, as the subject would be forwarded to proper authority. I felt as they did; it was wrong to exercise such authority over field personnel without having a feel for the pulse of the operation, an understanding of accomplishment, or for that matter and conversely the detrimental consequences of such a brazen self-serving undertaking it might have been. I was guessing cooler heads would prevail, and they did.

I reviewed the detail of the situation, emphasizing the concern of field management and their employees, with my immediate management. My recommendation was to curb the instruction or at least modify the questionnaire to detract from its pointed reference to education. It took but a few minutes to follow the rationale of my concern and I was asked to escort my manager to the office of the then division general manager, Lee Iacocca. I sat in his outer chambers until given a nod to enter. Much like the actions of Charlie Patterson, who ultimately became the company president, the writer of the questionnaire was summoned into Lee's office. It perhaps would have been better if I had stayed in the outer office. Quite properly, at least in my opinion, the manager responsible for the instructional release was torn apart, up one side and down another. There was comment that the writer was an overly educated imbecile and didn't know or understand people. This was followed by a few choice superlatives, ending with, "Write an immediate retraction of the communication to all locations informing them the direction was in error and was being rescinded." Lee Iacocca's instruction was followed to a tee. Our field locations and employees breathed a long sigh of relief when in short order they received the rescinding order. They knew who tightened the screws, and thanked me for the assistance. If the path for corrective action was other than I had predicted, we would have been left with a lot of disenchanted people waiting for the other shoe to fall.

Fortunately I had a notion that the general manager had never forgotten his beginnings and understood the personnel picture. I was right, but still to this day have misgivings as to where some of our underling head-liners, seeking unabashed glory, seem to be coming from.

The next time I remember seeing Lee Iacocca was at my friend Nick's father's funeral services. Nick was our cafeteria manager, who coincidentally was assigned to the central staff offices about the same time Lee took over the presidency of the company, and he, like so many of us, had a deep respect for the former general manager of our division. Even though I had worked for him and was responsible to him at a top organizational level, he didn't know me from a bale of hay and still doesn't. He took the time from his very demanding and busy schedule at the Glass House to pay his respects to the father of just another employee.

In a short period from having seen him last, I again was in the area of his company. At this time the setting was less than favorable in that his severance from the top position level of the company had been announced. Like one of his predecessors, he was being given the opportunity to occupy an office at our parts depot on Telegraph Road as a stop point before a total exiting. (This was the Depot I spoke of earlier, this extended facility occupied often by the Rouge plant.) He was in the building manager's office, which was next to the office he was to occupy. The question of coffee came up and together they proceeded to the vending machine, quite unlike the way he had become accustomed to having his coffee served over the many years. I was in the wings, and after he engaged in some small talk with the building manager Carl, he thanked him and left the building and never did occupy the designated office area. I was glad he left as he did and without giving the satisfaction of a fallen hero to Mr. Ford II, the man who in the minds of many, including myself, did him under.

As many people knew, Iacocca had toyed with several major opportunities after he left Ford. Chrysler, I don't believe, ever fully realized how lucky they were to get him. Here was a man who put them back on the map. Here was the guy who almost single-handedly convinced the United States government that it was imperative and in our total best interest that they acquiesce to a loan Chrysler was seeking, and only in that way could the rebuilding and rebirth of the organization be achieved. This was done, and the promise of repayment to the United States by Chrysler was also achieved.

One of his first Chrysler management association gatherings came shortly after he was announced as the new president. He planned a Detroit meeting with all his field management executives and those of the Detroit area. Here again, and backtracking for a minute, and unbeknown to him, I received a call from his and my friend Nick, telling me of the gala event that was in the planning stages, and all that was necessary to button it up was a first-class catering service capable of handling the requirements. Lee apparently had called Nick personally, and Nick called me. For some reason Nick recalled a conversation of many years before when we had worked out a contractual union agreement and I had for some reason mentioned several favorite Italian restaurants. His comment to me was that I had to help. He was unwilling to accept my comment that he rather than I was in the business and his selection would probably best serve the occasion. After considerable haggling, I directed Nick to a quality eating establishment, not with catering experience as such, but if they would be willing to handle the occasion, Lee would, I'm sure, be pleased. I did recall cautioning Nick of the tough area in which the restaurant was located, as well as the tough associated clientele, and asked him to handle his request delicately. I gave him the phone number and kept my fingers crossed that the contact would work out. Sure enough it did. The hangup that came into play, sometime after the festivities were over and effectively accomplished, and again directed to me via Nick, was the question of the amount to be charged, as the restaurant had never catered before and were not sure of the pricing. I reminded Nick I was not the expert in these matters, but did tell him not to have the caterer look a gift horse in the mouth, as this totally satisfactory initial experience, as I understood it, could lead to many more good business opportunities for the future. I lucked out once again in my recommendation and directions as the entire episode came to a finale. Suddenly a highly reputable and quality food restaurant became a catering establishment as well. My subsequent understanding was the agreed-upon pricing was right, and as a consequence requests for many more Chrysler dinner meetings and food service requirements were requested and favorably met. I was personally pleased that Lee was doing well, and from a distance, I could still make a contribution.

There are still two things that I may incorporate as a part of this book or may consider as a side bar or inside cover flap, relating to my phantom acquaintance with this man. The first of which relates to his daughter's wedding as well as separately to my daughter, and the arrangements that had been made for the entire wedding party to be driven to and from the ceremonies in a trolley. Well, the photographer and camera people, Marissa and Joe, at the Focal Point Studios of Farmington Hills, took the occasion to show the pictures of my daughter's pre-wedding ceremonies, including the trolley that had been used for the first time for the group's transportation to the church and back home. I thought the trolley idea was a good idea, as did my son-in-law-to-be, Rick, who worked out the details of the arrangement, and apparently so did the Iacocca family as they made the same photographic and transportation choice. I'm sure it worked out well for them as it did for us, and while this too is a departure from *Ford:*

An Era Remembered, we wish them all well and success in the future.

The second thing I'd like to take the liberty to mention, and this is for Lee, is the fact that I still have a few of the old management pictures of Lee and his organizational peers taken back in the Ford division days. By the way, I happened to drive by the engineering test track and sadly have to tell Lee that our Ford division building adjacent to the track was in the final stages of demolition. They did tear down the 3000 Schaefer Road building that I was last housed in, with Chet Barion and his division people, and I could with much displeasure understand the need there, but I'm hard pressed to understand the rationale associated with the tear-down of this relatively new structure, the designated Ford division structure. Maybe they call it progress. If by chance Lee happens to read this book and would like the copies I spoke of, he can get in touch with me in the Farmington Hills area, as I've lost track of his whereabouts since his move to the West Coast. Good luck to Lee and his family and continuing good health and success.

CHAPTER 28
OF SECURITY CONCERNS

With the ending of the Korean War, the Ford building program again got underway and the division facility (now in the throes of being demolished) was built on the site directly across from the test track area. The new building finally allowed at the time a consolidation of the division's components, which had been scattered across numerous facilities, as well as occupancy at outside leased locations. Like the experiences of many newly activated undertakings, this was no exception. Office locations, parking facilities, and safety and security features all had to be integrated with people understanding for an effective transition into the new mode of operation. I had been reassigned several times during this period, and one of my added responsibilities included safety and security of the new building. Having had some knowledge and background, again it wasn't too difficult to meld the added responsibility into my normal routine. In short order, and as another of my favorite recollections, I had been requested to meet with members of our engineering staff, who reported stock losses, and suspected thieves in one of their metal-fabricating shops. My surveillance of the area, with numerous follow-up visits, caused me to conclude the work in progress was being maintained at an unusually accelerated and orderly pace with each of the separate stations apparently doing their assigned work. What didn't fit the pattern was where the bulk of the finished work was routed to. Not to belabor the point, it was determined the effort going into the work was not solely for the company's benefit, but in one instance for personal gain. It seemed that one of the employees took it upon himself to work on his Airstream trailer. He was very busy at his workstation, panel by panel and section by section, and for all purposes was credited as an excellent employee. The kicker was, his work was for personal gain and his supervision didn't know the difference, or at least that was what I had been led to believe. He conveniently stored his unfinished pieces of sheet metal over the offices within the area that his supervisor occupied, and the next day resumed his activity by falling in line with the other metal workers. His exiting from his work area and building was relatively simple, under the guise of transporting finished work to an adjacent building, conveniently en route to his residence. He was caught, while management and his immediate supervision are perhaps still wondering how he got away with his little game, right under their noses and red faces, with his hiding place actually right above their heads. I never did find out how many Airstream trailers this highly talented employee had built, but with his enterprising capabilities, without being supervised, he should have been able to make a comfortable added income. It is undoubtedly difficult to visualize how this could have happened, but in the engineering center with the many hands-on operations, under the caption "experimental," coupled with a mix of supervision and free thinkers, it did happen, and in all likelihood in certain instances probably still does.

It was during this launching period of the then new building that the test track directly across from the building was having their annual model airplane meet, open to the various model airplane clubs throughout the country, and on the grounds where Mr. Ford had launched his initial interest in air flight. Model planes of all sizes and shapes, carefully handled by the owners along with their sons or daughters, were competing for design, performance, and related trophies. It was obvious many hours of time and talent had gone into the fabrication of these beautiful pieces of art. The planes were propelled by gasoline engines and were flown via remote control. All the gyrations were directed from the ground control of the owners. It was a beautiful thing to see from the upper floors of our new building. Unfortunately there was a disaster associated with the meet. The planes without warning were crashing into the ground or into one another without the least understanding of what was going on.

This heartbreaking scenario for many of the competitors brought into need a call for security personnel as well as the local police to determine the source or sources responsible. It was believed that youngsters had either penetrated the enclosed engineering test track area where the competition was being held and through some source were inflicting the damage, or perhaps getting on the top sections of the protective walls and using BB guns to knock down the airborne models. While the security people of the test track had encircled the outer walls with several modes of security, no evidence of intentional sabotage was uncovered. Now here comes the answer.

As already mentioned, we were a new facility in a beautiful five-story building, and many innovative features were introduced with the occupancy of the building. One of the features introduced for our maintenance supervision and building maintenance employees was the new communication system, between supervision and their employees, via a two-way walkie-talkie radio hookup. This was new and highly efficient in contacting and directing the employee or work effort. The system was new in the company as it was in this new building. You've probably guessed the downfall of the untried communication system by now, but if you haven't the answer lies in the frequency the communication system had been authorized to use by the company, and that of the model plane enthusiasts. Once a contact had to be made between supervision and employee via the new walkie-talkie communication system, the flight of the model planes was cut off. No problems had existed previously during the meets and the sudden surge of mishaps was a surprise to the sponsors, the police, and above all the competitors. A solution was quite simple once the cause had been determined. A change in frequency usage resolved all the problems. Now for all I know the meets continue to be held under Ford sponsorship and on the restricted frequency allocated for the model airplane enthusiasts alone. We've sure come a long way since the advent of the walkie-talkie.

CHAPTER 29
MANAGER SIDE-STEPPING RESPONSIBILITY

W e can go on, now that we're talking frequencies, with another happening behind closed doors that I was directed to resolve. It seemed that a young ambitious public relations type with direct access to the new general manager of the division—this was subsequent to Lee Iacocca's appointment to the Ford central staff level—convinced the then general manager that the need for improved design and forward planning secrecy was needed in his office and in the contacts with guests and business associates. According to my understanding, the young associate was overpowered with the thought of industrial espionage running rampant in the auto industry, and alluded to a need for measures to be taken to prevent such an occurrence within the general manager's office. Typically my manager responded without an understanding or meaning of the issue, indicating he would take care of the problem. And, as in many situations before, the solution was not of his doing but rather passing the buck, regardless of substance, to me. His rationale was that I was responsible for security and therefore I had to come up with the answers. It is best that I not mention names at this juncture. I was totally annoyed. Mind you, this whole stream of nonsense began with an idiot comment that something should be done in the general manager's office. I had no escaping the far-out assignment. After trying to convince my evasive leader, without success, that someone's imagination was getting the best of him, I had to follow the lead he had stupidly volunteered for. Well, here again as in my past, cornering assignments, my mind was operating full-tilt and I wasn't about to let him off lightly. I informed him I would lay out my plan and required total acceptance before proceeding. The next morning it went something like this: I will need the building security officer in charge to work with me and have his photographic equipment available, I want the manager of office services present, and above all I will need the secretary of the general manager to be present during our weekend invasion of his office, to observe what was taking place. All of this was to be done on overtime and when, for all purposes, the building was empty, and there was no interference by unionized personnel. If they became involved, then related monetary grievances were to be paid.

My terms were understood and met. The personnel assignments were lined up, date and time was set, and my cloak-and-dagger episode was in place. My manager felt it best that he not be present. I preferred it that way. We met in the designated office with all involved present. My security man brought his camera, and also obtained an electronic sound finder which was to detect any frequency waves being emitted from a planted eaves-dropping apparatus. We began our search of the entire office, bookcases, desk, ceiling, and closets. I asked the secretary to do nothing but observe and comment if the papers, books, etc., were not returned in their original order. With a tall ladder, brought in the night before, we were able to scan the inner-ceiling areas, as we were also able, through the listening device, to check where a bug could most likely be planted. We went through a very extensive search while knowing down deep that this piece of electronics wasn't about to find a thing. A costly exercise in futility was in the making, and anything less would not have made my manager satisfied with my conclusions. The security officer was asked to continue taking pictures until satisfied all angles had been covered. He, along with the others involved, also suspected, as I did, a full-blossomed witch-hunt. However, cooperating to the fullest extent, he did for what it was worth a very commendable job. It is well to point out that I had discussed this request with my central staff counterpart, who recommended against the idea, indicating that if we began to suspect goblins, we'd have to check behind walls, floors, flower beds, terraces, and bathrooms throughout the company, and this was not a recommended undertaking. I informed them of the prevailing attitudes and nothing less than a run at surveillance effort was in the offing. With their blessing, but not their endorsement, I was able to proceed with the charade.

We literally tore the office apart, restroom and adjacent anteroom included. We checked floors and ceiling as well as standing floral arrangements. There was nothing observed nor was there a beep from our automatic equipment. While this was going on the secretary was observing all, and our photographer was recording our every move. I finally called it quits for the group. The setting was returned as it was found and acknowledged as such by our observer, the secretary. The following day the ladders were removed and the general manager was none the wiser. I informed my manager of the happenings over the weekend, telling him I'd have a written report for his perusal and disposition. Included in the book report were several of the photographs which literally depicted the surveillance activity undertaken, with a copy of my cover letter confirming no covert actions nor intrusive were known to have been undertaken or found as a result of our findings. Our pictures served effectively, truly worth over a thousand spoken words. Typically, there was no spoken word of appreciation for an assignment undertaken by myself, my appointed group, and definitely satisfactorily completed. My materials were routed by the man taking the bows to the division general manager and this issue was closed. Those of us participating knew our mission had been successfully completed and it was I that told them so. By the way, our young and exuberant whistle blower in this instance had left the employ of the company and with less than favorable exiting.

While still somewhat chagrined at the less than

Ford Motor Company

Intra-Company Communication

C O N F I D E N T I A L

September 13, 1966

In accordance with our conversation, a security review of Mr. Frey's office was conducted on Monday, September 12, by the writer, Mr. C. M. Stout and Mr. R. C. McCormick, Ford Division Security Supervisor.

The purpose of the review was to assure the area being surveyed was free of devices customarily used in espionage activity such as microphones (room-bugs), built-in recording devices, or other eavesdropping equipment. The area shown in the attached office layout was completely probed. The examination of bookcases, cabinets, desks, worktables and those items of a personal nature was conducted in the presence of Mr. Frey's secretary.

In addition to the search for any electrical recording or transmitting devices, the possibility of radio transmission or recording equipment was ruled out by the use of an electronic transmitter detector scanning instrument obtained for this investigation. The electronic unit is an instrument designed to detect high frequency radio transmission.

We believe this security review affords reasonable assurance that the area in question is free of any of the generally considered eavesdropping devices at this time. In the event another such review is deemed necessary, we have prepared photographs (enclosed) of the activity undertaken during this review which may be compared with subsequent investigative materials to possibly detect changes and to perhaps ascertain the time period during which espionage activity, if any, occurred.

O. J. Nori
Hourly Personnel, Labor Relations,
Safety and Security Manager

Concur:

C. M. Stout, Manager
Administrative Services Department

R. C. McCormick, Supervisor
Security Section
Administrative Services Department

177

people-oriented attitude of my manager on more than one occasion, there was still another interesting development which occurred.

Apart from the above, and on a separate occasion, I was called into my manager's office and informed out of the blue that it was to be my responsibility to fire a long-time salaried employee for theft. While I knew and understood my responsibilities in the area of security, I knew nothing of the activity which he alluded to, or, for that matter, that which had been identified as theft. Written investigative reporting and the related written documentation coming into our division was not shared but rather kept under strict secrecy by our office manager. He was again playing games with his importance and authority until it became too hot to handle further. I was informed, after the fact, that the theft amongst other things involved the improper disposition of company prototype vehicles entrusted for demolition and scrapping, as well as the releasing of prototype cars and trucks to several unauthorized and unknown persons. The person in the hot seat that I was being told to fire was a former associate of mine in charge of security and plant protection at the parts distribution center, whom I had worked with for many years. Without providing me with times and places, I was told that he had in fact loaned out the vehicles, without authorization, to neighboring farm owners, for their use within the boundaries of their properties, with understanding that they would be returned for demolition at a specified time. The number of units involved, the location of his neighboring farm owners, or how the trucks or cars were being used was left without answers. Obviously I was surprised. The man in question was a very active member, as were his children, in the 4-H club activities. He was known to have done a lot for his community, and I couldn't fathom for a moment that his involvement was without the knowledge of his next-in-line authority, or authorized with understanding as to where the units were, and their intended ultimate disposition.

I was being told by my manager of my responsibilities within the realm of my security functions, however in this case only after the fact, and obviously in only selected territory. I didn't like it. I'd had about enough of this repetitively displayed superiority and aloofness. I informed him I wasn't even remotely apprised of the happenings, and as the management person on his staff I should have been. Further, if I wasn't to be informed, and with some semblance of confidence, then he didn't need me. The person whom I was to take such action against was a friend, and I couldn't and wouldn't unilaterally fire the man. Secondly, the responsibility for the dismissal of this significantly higher-level salaried individual fell directly on him to execute, as the staff manager, rather than myself. Also, if my responsibilities included the dismissal of persons within the organization without my personal prior knowledge or understanding of the facts, then I didn't know that. I was hot and didn't much care. I informed him under the circumstances the actions he sought were his, not mine. He didn't like it, and at that moment I didn't care. His next port of call was with our salaried personnel manager, who perhaps should have been his first calling, as he was the division's designated salaried people overseer, not me.

He too was told by our manager of the actions sought, and here again the response was negative as both our manager of salaried personnel and the man in question lived in the same community as neighbors. Somewhere along the line I believe I had mentioned, absent division-level direct actions, the responsibility would have been, or should have been, appropriately handled by his immediate management and not footballing the issue in favor of having others execute the directive. I felt I was giving my manager a lesson in proper organizational line and staff responsibilities, something he should have known about, but often times I wondered. Again, I was not kept in tune with the final happenings but concluded the facility manager was given the duty, and that the security supervisor of the parts distribution center, along with others under his jurisdiction, had lost their jobs. His personal appeals to upper central staff management for position retention were apparently in vain. The responsibility for firing the man was shuffled around until finally I believe it was delegated to the facility manager, who took the removal actions. That which did occur in this instance, as a result of the dismissal, was a helping hand, via his staff management mentor, for an assignment to an even better position with Chrysler. Politics played a strange hand in this concluding case disposition. It seemed to portray that the one who got to the central staff office with their case scenario first won all the marbles. Ira's mentor was not, unfortunately, the first at the staff level to be apprised of the situation, therefore he lost. Ira disappeared from the Ford scene. I didn't see him again, nor did I ever have the opportunity to hear his side of the story. Our paths, as is often the case in the automobile industry, had gone their separate directions many years before. Knowing him as I did, there just had to be greater and more favorable detail than that reported in the investigative findings. I was pleased for him and his family that his recovery would surface, and the Ford experience, as unpleasant as it was, would be overshadowed for him in time with better things at Chrysler. Long after the terminating actions, I was told that a neighboring lady farm owner was calling the Ford Motor Company to determine her final handling of the vehicle that had been loaned to her for use on her farm.

I know I'm coming across with negativity toward the man I was working for, but that's the way it was. I had been taught that if you can't say something nice about a person, don't say anything. Unfortunately throughout our association his preferred actions were with those assigned to him having a background as he did, only in salaried personnel matters. As I saw it, he had no love whatever for anyone associated with the hourly workforce, or the union/company relationships. I personally concluded he didn't know or understand the field and had a hard time in comprehending the rationale. While I was fortunate enough to have had both sides of the experience ledger, I had handled his favorite area of endeavor long before it became an entity unto itself. It was most difficult to convince or attempt an education into a field of least interest for him, and unfortunately I felt our relationship, because of my responsibilities and his background, was stressful. I realistically cannot hold to the adage, "say nothing," as I was doing a job to benefit both my well-being and his. Unfortunately we were of differing backgrounds and traveling a different path. This will happen in an organization as large and complex as ours. So be it, and I wasn't about to lose sleep over it.

As a consequence of reorganization, I was assigned to the newly created operation, with responsibility for eighteen field and metropolitan area locations, its personnel activities, including the labor relations functions. More interesting was the fact that my former manager recommended me for the promotional reassignment, concluding that he was appreciative of our relationship, and for the better understanding he had gained in the field I had dedicated most of my working life toward. The experience gained in my new and independent entity was most gratifying for me, as I was able to make the final recommendations in the area of responsibility I was charged with and see them executed within the operation, and above all having a unique relationship with Galen, the assigned operations manager, who gave me carte blanche authorization in the handling of the activities I had been given responsibility for. I never said much to him nor did he to me, but I effectively operated under an invisible veil of respect for the man and in turn, trust.

CHAPTER 30
MECHANIZED PROCESSING
AND REAL PROGRESS

Recently, I took the time to reread my notes, knowing well that because of the lengthy time span between my writings, there was more than one occasion to repeat my situation experiences in this chronology. I'm sure there are repeats, however the condensations and passage elimination will just have to wait until the complete scenario is finished and then appropriately edited. For now, and still in the absence of an outline customarily used for publication and appropriate coverage purposes, I'm going on with this factual portrayal of what I recall were some of the highlights of these lengthy and, I do believe, important experiences. For those of you who have tolerated me thus far, I'm not too far from ending this story, and hopefully it has been of some value to you. I could go on and cite the hundreds of labor relations cases I personally handled, and with mild exception resolved effectively and for the benefit of most. There are also the many disciplinary cases referred for resolution, each of which being a story unto itself, however best left at this time to memory and a thing of the past. It is necessary to point out that the age of computerization was coming into play during my experiences in the parts operations.

It was during this time that the conflict with the local union arose, beginning with their demands to bring in and install the giant computer cabinetry from the receiving docks to the specially prepared and equipped computer rooms. Keep in mind this was the beginning of automation, and considerable experimentation was going on. We were able to effectively convince the union representation that the equipment and its installation was under contract, and only qualified technicians from the vendor were authorized to make the delivery and handle the equipment to its intended final location and installation point; anything less would have been cause to void the whole contract.

What appears to have been resolved by two or three sentences above did realistically take a considerable amount of convincing time. It really came down to either the vending company handling the installation completely or going for an installation elsewhere. The union representation finally realized the error of their ways and relented. They came to realize that failure to accept the position that I had outlined could in short order detrimentally affect greater incoming work requests and in turn increased work volumes for their constituency.

The conflicts in the transformation to mechanized handling didn't end with the incoming equipment but rather carried through with what at the time was a far-out union position that the hourly employee should be the persons schooled and operating the equipment. This too had to be resolved, and it took an umpire to arbitrate final understanding and resolution of the differences. The equipment operations were left up to trained and qualified technical programmers and salaried persons who were in tune with the progression and forward strides the mechanized equipment was bringing into play for the company and industry as a whole. This wasn't to say an hourly person couldn't be trained in some phase of mechanization, but the timing wasn't right.

It wasn't an easy task to get the union representatives to understand the concepts of mechanized handling. I recall discussing the need to introduce the system for trained salaried people in the first instance to the national headquarters of the union. To assist in convincing them of the complicated features of the equipment already brought in and limitedly operating, I recall telling them of one of the breakdowns occurring in our attempts to get the equipment to effectively operate online. The breakdown was traced to a little mouse who had somehow gotten into the highly sophisticated wired room and was electrocuted within the maze of wiring in the computer. This little true story went a long way, as I remember inviting the union's national Ford department hierarchy for a visit to witness first-hand the installation and the beginnings of what is now a highly complex and advanced operation. The representation came to our location with their associates and I accompanied them to the computer rooms. These were the huge reel-to-reel cabinets with many lights, buzzers, and minimal personnel operators. They were carried through the operating features by one of the attendants and shown how the equipment operated. It was during this show-and-tell episode that I had overheard one of the representatives telling one of his associates of the little mouse, and wanting to know if this was where the tragedy occurred.

The growth of the computer age for us from the manual operations to computerization was a long and difficult trail. Fortunately we kept abreast of the fast-moving technology and salvaged entry into the advanced stages of its use, through the cooperation and understanding of the union representatives at their higher offices.

EPILOGUE

As I browse through this small recap of life, I am reminded there are many more incidents to incorporate for the reader, but like all things, this too must come to an end. I believe I covered enough to give the reader an understanding of the heartaches, pitfalls, and varied accomplishments. I do this for the benefit of the next generation, leading them to hopefully understand that achievement is possible but it won't be served up to you. You have to follow your dream and above all you must stick with some thoughts of your plan. I believe I did this, and I know that I now can look back with thoughts of gratitude and satisfaction. There in fact were many highs and lows in what today is referred to as a career. There were many members of management that I wish I hadn't encountered in this career. I may have already alluded to one or more and if I expressed negative thinking toward them, I strongly feel they had it coming and I don't alter or negate my comments. Conversely there were many more able and qualified managers and supervisors that I had the good fortune to become associated with, and I'm thankful for having had the opportunity to have worked for and with them in the various assignment responsibilities.

The peaks and valleys in personalities is something I had no control of, and the same expectations could possibly be true with others who would be willing to venture a career path as I undertook. To a great extent, the path I took was a necessity of the times, and once given the opportunity, you stuck with it or were out. Today, fortunately for the youngsters, there are a multitude of opportunities. There are no police horses controlling the long lines of employment seekers, and the beautiful thing is if you don't like what you have signed up for, you can leave for greener pastures.

I apologize if by the mention of certain names or references I mischaracterized their well-being. I wish to extend my thanks to the members of my family, including the grandkids, who on more than one occasion gave me a quick lesson in computer technology, allowing me to proceed toward this end. As a final reminder this book is an insight for the benefit of my wife, who tolerated my ups and downs over the years, for my family for sharing in my good and bad times, and finally, for the youngsters reading this book, allowing better understanding of what can be ahead for them and how to anticipate and prepare for their own future. I began this writing with an objective of presenting an overview of my factual slice of life, portraying for the reader what can be expected in traveling through a career. I believe I've accomplished this, and the reader will benefit by the detail provided for his or her purposes. I also believe I've characterized the pitfalls one can expect, as well as some of the more favorable highlights. Totally, this experience wasn't a piece of cake, but ended, fortunately, quite well for me. I've still got my health, I've a nice home and family, and how else can one measure success in this maze that we live in? Hopefully, by your reading and in anticipation of what may be in store for you, you too will be rewarded and life will serve you better. With much success, I am O. J. Nori, the writer of this long recapitulation of life in time and place. If you wish to seek greater insights, like I said to Mr. Iacocca, I'm in the phone book and I'd like to hear from you.

My personal and ending regards.